PETER AND MAGDALEN

Peter and Magdalen

The Gospel Runs in Two Voices

Damiano Marzotto

Translated by Mark Paver and Anne Monckton

GRACEWING

First published in Italian as
Pietro e Maddalena. Il vangelo corre a due voci
by
ÀNCORA EDITRICE,
Via G.B. Niccolini, 8
20154 Milano
Italy
© 2010 ÀNCORA EDITRICE

English edition first published in 2015
by
Gracewing
2 Southern Avenue
Leominster
Herefordshire HR6 0QF
United Kingdom
www.gracewing.co.uk

English translation by Mark Paver and Anne Monckton
© 2015 Damiano Marzotto

ISBN 978 085244 874 8

Typeset by Gracewing

Cover design by Bernardita Peña Hurtado,
incorporating detail from Carlo Crivelli, *St Catherine of Alexandria,
St Peter, and St Mary Magdalene*, c. 1475, wood panels, Santa
Lucia, Montefiore dell'Aso, Italy.

CONTENTS

INTRODUCTION

Men and Women serving the Gospel

CO-OPERATION IN THE work of the Gospel has always seen men and women working together, engaged in a common, passionate and continuing effort in fidelity to the Lord (cf Phil 4:2; Rom 16). This was the case not only at the time of Paul, but has been verified through the course of centuries and is certainly no less true today. Nevertheless, in this respect certain questions can be raised and certain problems have yet to be resolved. Above all there is a regrettable lack of visibility of women in the Church and in evangelization.

Therefore, when attempts are made to give substance to a more qualified presence of women, it is not always clear whether the task simply involves a redistribution of roles traditionally attributed to men or whether room is truly being made for feminine originality, thereby enriching the entire Church and the world. Moreover, it is also true that men do not always have a clear awareness of the particular vocation of the woman, especially in the ecclesial sphere. Often the woman is considered as only a secondary figure, more readily available for humble roles, and the unique contribution to evangelization and enrichment of the Church and society she possesses is not appreciated. These considerations demonstrate how a more general and fundamental question emerges here.

In other words, whether serving evangelization and, in general, serving the life of the Church a better collaboration between men and women might not only be appropriate but even necessary. Once this question is formulated and a generic positive response is given, the practical arrangements for this desired collaboration need to be clarified so as to make the best of the gifts of both men and women.

Indeed, for a number of years now, I have embarked upon an analytical research of the New Testament, with the publication of some articles relating to the Synoptic Gospels, the Acts of the Apostles and St John's Gospel. While each essay was published with different goals I realized that they constitute a fairly coherent and comprehensive framework in that they represent the perspectives of the four evangelists. It seemed therefore worthwhile to publish them together in a single volume.

My research has led me to understand all the more that, if the general perspective of the New Testament is one of evangelization, the broadening of horizons, and moving towards a universal unity in Christ, such dynamics of salvation were actually accomplished — therefore is accomplished and can be accomplished — in a synergy between male and female.

What are the common lines that characterize this collaboration and which are found, even if with different emphases, in the New Testament books?

There seem to be three fundamental issues:

1. A receptive ability on the part of the woman that goes alongside a greater activism on the part of the man. Above all in Matthew and in Luke there is evidence that the divine initiative is received with greater depth and interior

freedom by women. This allows for the maturation and safe custody of the message. The woman's capacity to listen and contemplate favours this deep penetration of the salvific event; the transforming reception of the Spirit. On the other hand, this receptive capacity is integrated, at a fundamental level, with actions completed by men, such as: giving the name to the new born, bringing the body of Jesus from the cross, becoming re-acquainted with the risen Jesus, and confronting with renewed effort their difficult mission.

2. A capacity of anticipation on the part of the woman, that precedes and prefigures successive male acts both in service and in the expansion of perspectives, in the faith as in the gift of self, in the intuition of the truth that saves, in the memory of the word of the Lord as announcement. Moreover, women are the ones who at times act in provocation in front of Jesus or of the apostles to lead them to a salvific act.

3. An emphasis towards the universal characterizes the interventions, often anticipatory, of the woman compared to the man. The mission is invited to grow; it is driven beyond the boundaries already outlined. With her simple presence, with a practical initiative or with specific verbal requests, the woman takes the mission beyond codified limits and enlarges its horizons. In every case, though, there is an asymmetric collaboration in which the two actors offer something which is differentiated and complementary.

It should be noted, finally, how, in this co-operation in the work of salvation, the virginal condition of the woman is emphasized. This situation, perhaps exactly in as much as it is a sign of poverty, fragility, and availability seems particularly adapted to receive the action of the Holy Spirit, the fertile Word and, at the moment of the Passion, the Body of the Saviour. At the same time, the virginal condition having allowed a more profound interiorisation, seems more capable of promoting a renewal and an expansion of the initiative of salvation.

To summarize briefly, if on the one hand the woman provokes, anticipates, receives, assimilates, deepens and therefore allows for a wider and more universal growth of the message of salvation; on the other hand the man carries to completion with timely, practical acts of restoration, and mercy, announcing that which was begun. As can be seen, the activity of the man needs a feminine counterpoint of interiorisation, of original and anticipatory effort, of ever greater openness without which the activity becomes activism and the impetus of the Gospel slows down and fades.

Today, as in the beginning, the action of the Church cannot be if it is not multiform, with different approaches, in a process of circulating stimuli, with mutual support. From this perspective, even priestly ordination being reserved to men could serve to better appreciate the specific contribution of the woman, a contribution expressed in other ways of presence and action, in order to prevent homogenisation to male models and in order not to deprive the Church, and all of humanity, of a contribution that is original and necessary.

ABBREVIATIONS

BEThL =   *Bibliotheca Ephemeridum Theologicarum Lovaniensium*

NRT =   *La nouvelle revue théologique*

NTD =   *Das Neue Testament Deutsch*

NTS =   *New Testament Studies*

PG =   *Patrologia Graeca*

Riv Bibl It = *Rivista Biblica [organo dell' Associazione biblica italiana]*

ZNW =   *Zeitschrift für die neutestamentliche Wissenschaft*

1

THE CELIBACY OF JESUS AND THE VIRGINITY OF MARY[1]

N THE NEW Testament Jesus is not spoken of explicitly as 'celibate'. Rather, Jesus is presented in the biblical perspective as the Mediator of the blessing of Abraham on the people (Gal 3:14), and Author of life (Acts 3:15). For an understanding of the unique celibacy of Jesus, it seems appropriate to attempt to shed light on how the evangelists presented his profile, 'first born of every creature', in reference to the original blessing of Genesis: 'Male and female he created them […] and he said to them: 'Be fertile and multiply'.

Matthew

The first Gospel begins with a phrase that holds great significance from the point of view of the 'status' of Jesus: 'Biblos geneseos Jesou Christou, uiou David, uiou Abraam…' ('Book of the genealogy of Jesus Christ, son of David, son of Abraham') (Mt 1:1). 'In the Septuagint, Biblos geneseos and like expressions introduce an individual, his descendents and not infrequently events.'[2] In fact however in what follows in the gospel of Matthew, we hear nothing of the sons of Jesus and neither of a woman from whom he would be able to have them.

This title of the Gospel of Matthew, however, is not void of content. All of the Gospel in fact tells us of how Jesus progressively turns towards the inhabitants of Palestine to make them disciples, right up to the conclusion of the Gospel (28:18ff), in which the risen Jesus sends the 11 disciples to 'make disciples of all the people [*panta ta ethne*], baptizing them in the name of the Father and of the Son and of the Holy Spirit'. In this way the promise made to Abraham, of whom Jesus himself is a descendent (Mt 1:1), is realized: 'In you all the people of the earth will be blessed' (Gen 12:3).[3]

It is also possible to translate the opening words of the Gospel of Matthew as follows: 'Book of the offspring of Jesus Christ...' In this way all of the work of salvation of Jesus is placed under the sign of generation, of the gift of a life, under the sign of the creation, as the obvious reference to the first chapters of Genesis invites us to do, in particular to verses 5:1 ('This is the book of the genealogy of Adam') and 2:4a ('These are the generations of the heavens and the earth when they were created.').[4] In Matthew though we are dealing with a new creation as the presence of the Spirit in 1:18ff testifies and as also the command to baptize 'in the name of the Father and of the Son and of the Holy Spirit', confirms in Mt 28:19.

In Genesis the theme of the genealogy is linked to that of the woman, Eve, the first woman. In reality Jesus is also born of a woman, of Mary, but in an extraordinary way, a way that the maternity of the four women mentioned in his genealogy had prepared and that the story of Mt 1:18–25 illustrates well: a virginal maternity made fertile by the Holy Spirit. The extraordinary modality of his birth from a woman, in the Holy Spirit, thus also prepares for the type of extraordinary relationship (in the Spirit) that Jesus lived with certain female figures, of whom he availed in order to carry out his work of salvation: so that the blessing of Abraham might pass in Him to all of the people.

In order to understand this affirmation, we need to recall how Matthew, in his story of the work of Jesus, presented certain female figures beginning with Mary of Nazareth, continuing up until the women under the cross and beside the tomb. Right at the centre of the Gospel, in the heart of the *'discourse on the parables'* (ch.13), a brief parable is found, the Woman of the Leaven (Mt 13:33). From this centre point, this parable casts light on the different figures of women that the evangelist introduces throughout his account of Jesus' life: 'The Kingdom of heaven is like a fist of leaven which a woman collected with joy and hid in three measures of flour until all [the world] was leavened'.

The leaven is the teaching, the word of Jesus, that he came to plant, and that the woman received with joy as the earth receives the seed.[5] The leaven has in itself a free and fertile force, like the Holy Spirit that rendered Mary the mother of the Saviour. The woman, after having collected the leaven, hid it inside an enormous quantity of flour (almost 36 litres). From a certain point of view it is a total removal of the leaven from view, but this is exact because it must be put into the heart of the pasta in order to leaven it. It is an enormous quantity of pasta to be leavened. The Gospel reaches the entire world[6], through this mystery of death, burial and new life. This was prophetically demonstrated by the woman at Bethany who anointed the head and body of Jesus with ointment in view of his upcoming burial 'All the world' will speak of that which she has done in memory of her.

Moreover, the encounter with the Canaan woman, and with the greatness of her faith, had pushed Jesus to broaden his mission beyond the lost sheep of the house of Israel;[7] just as the faith of the haemorrhaging woman had caused Jesus to make a gift to her of salvation, so entirely unexpected for a woman in such an impure condition.[8]

Above all though there is a special participation of women in the mystery of the death and resurrection of Jesus:

> And Jesus cried again with a loud voice and yielded up his spirit. And behold, the curtain of the temple was torn in two, from top to bottom; and the earth shook, and the rocks were split; the tombs also were opened, and many bodies of the saints who had fallen asleep were raised, and coming out of the tombs after his resurrection they went into the holy city and appeared to many. When the centurion and those who were with him, keeping watch over Jesus, saw the earthquake and what took place, they were filled with awe, and said, 'Truly this was the Son[a] of God!'
>
> There were also many women there, looking on from afar, who had followed Jesus from Galilee, ministering to him; among whom were Mary Magdalen, and Mary the mother of James and Joseph, and the mother of the sons of Zebedee. [...]And Joseph took the body, and wrapped it in a clean linen shroud, and laid it in his own new tomb [...] Mary Mag'dalene and the other Mary were there, sitting opposite the sepulchre. (Mt 27:50–61)

Here there is an interior participation in the mystery of the death and of the burial in the tomb that is nevertheless resonant and fraught with all the fruitfulness of the Spirit, sent by the dying Christ.

Indeed this persevering contemplation of the tomb ('toward the dawn of the first day of the week, Mary Magdalen and the other Mary went to see the sepulchre' (Mt 28:1)) is halted by the announcement of the angel ('he is risen') and by the encounter with Jesus himself ('Do not be afraid; go and tell my brethren to go to Galilee; and there they will see me.'). And it is in Galilee that Jesus says: 'Go therefore and make disciples of all nations'. The leaven that transforms the world was received, interiorized, hidden in the depths and therefore released all of its potentiality. 'His [the angel's] appearance was like lightning, and his raiment white as snow.' (Mt 28:3).

The mission of Jesus seemed to have substantially failed on the evening of Holy Thursday when all of his disciples had fled, abandoning him.[9] Nevertheless at the end of chapter 28 (v.16) we find that the eleven had returned to Galilee 'to the mountain to which Jesus had directed them.' This reversal of the situation was made possible by the small group of women that had followed Jesus from Galilee, that were present at the death of Jesus on the cross, at the burial, at the tomb again on the first day of the week, and to whom, finally, Jesus said, 'go and tell my brethren to go to Galilee, and they will see me.' Following these directions the eleven disciples returned to Galilee and there they were given the universal mission. The circle is closed, the communication between Jesus and his 'brothers' is re-established; the mission of Jesus did not come to nothing, but rather, it is from here that everything begins anew.

Furthermore, if one considers more closely the presentation of these women of the Passion that Matthew gives us, one cannot but be struck by the delicate yet precise comparison that he establishes with the figure of Mary, the mother of Jesus. Not only are these women, as we have already observed, made fertile by the Spirit, but in Mt 27–28, as in the narration of the 'genesis' of Jesus Christ (1:18–25), we can identify three stages of an extraordinary birth.

It is well-known that the story of Matthew 1:18–25 returns with insistence to the three affirmations that mark the prophecy of Isaiah: 'Behold, a virgin shall conceive/ and bear a son/ and his name shall be called Emmanuel.'[10] Now, as in Mt 27–28, after Jesus gives up His Spirit, while the women were looking on from afar, reference is made to Joseph of Arimathea who placed the body of Jesus in his tomb which is specified to be 'new'.[11] After Joseph rolled a great stone to the door of the tomb the narration ends saying: 'Mary Magdalen and the other Mary were there, sitting opposite the sepulchre.' (Mt 27:61). This new monument, cut into the rock, is like a new 'virginal' womb that opens itself to receive and protect in the memory, of the women first of all, the body of the crucified one.[12]

Indeed this 'new virginal womb' does not close forever on the body of Jesus, but these women that had assisted in the reposition of the body are the same that return to continue their contemplation of the tomb ('*theoresai ton taphon*', 28:1), they are in fact witnesses of its opening, of the great earthquake, of the removal of the rock that had been covering the entrance to the tomb and above all they receive the announcement,

'He is not here, for he has risen […] and behold, he is going before you to Galilee' (Mt 28:7). There is thus almost a new birth. The women that had contemplated the death of Jesus on the cross; that had assisted at his burial in a sense receiving Him into their own deepest interior, now take part in his re-birth into the world in a context of apocalyptic upheaval that mimics the travails of an eschatological birth.[13]

Finally, it is by following the direction given to the women by the risen Jesus Himself, that the disciples, reassembled in Galilee, hear the reassuring concluding words, 'and lo, I am with you always, to the close of the age.' (Mt 28:20). With this comes the fulfilment of the prophecy recalled by the angel: 'His name shall be called Emmanuel (which means God with us).' (Mt 1:23).

As we will see, this suggestive parallel between the Annunciation of the Messiah and His passion is present also in Luke, but in any case, it seems that for Matthew a state of fertile virginity is not a reality limited to the mother of Jesus, but may be also, in a more symbolic way, extended to other women who — by their particular participation in the death and resurrection of the Lord, comprised of contemplation, participation, offering of a particular, reserved space — make a figure of virginity 'in the Spirit', particularly adapted to the reception and the 'regeneration' of the crucified Jesus. From this point of view, it is significant that in the eschatological discourse Matthew presents 10 virgins ('*parthenoi*')[14] as models of vigilance required by Jesus, that contrast with the attitude of those unprepared who, as the flood came near, were eating and drinking, marrying and giving in marriage.[15]

We can now deepen our understanding of those to whom Jesus sent the women with his message: 'the eleven disciples'. They are the ones to whom Jesus entrusted the mission to 'make disciples' of all nations (Mt 28:19). They are those that Jesus intimately involves in his mission to give life to all the nations, 'baptizing them in the name of the Father and of the Son and of the Holy Spirit'. This task of adding to the discipleship of Jesus (*'matheteusate'*), baptizing them and teaching them 'all that I commanded you' will ensure that the blessing of Abraham can pass to 'all the nations'. Thus life is truly given to the descendents of Jesus Christ, son of David, son of Abraham.

Jesus entrusted to the eleven here a task that is extremely particular: that of continuing to 'make disciples': that is to add to Him new people capable of continuing the experience of discipleship after his death and resurrection. It is noted that the verb *'matheteuo'* recurs elsewhere only in Mt 27:57: 'a rich man from Arimathea, named Joseph, who was also [made a] disciple [*matheteuo*] of Jesus'. We have here then an inclusion. If, before Easter, it was Jesus who 'made disciples', after Easter it is the eleven who 'make disciples'; there is therefore an engagement of the disciples on the part of Jesus in a role that renders them totally in solidarity with a specific mission: through the eleven that had seen the Risen One, Jesus continues to 'make disciples', 'every day until the close of the age.'

This task in reality is nothing but the repetition of that given by Jesus to these men at the beginning of His ministry, when He called some intimately to His mission. First of all we must remember the calls of the two sets of brothers (Mt 4:18–22). Jesus had said: 'Follow me, and I will make you fishers of men'; and leaving their nets, their boat and their father they followed Him. It is thus indicated that the discipleship of Jesus has a specific goal, the participation in his mission of eschatological gathering, and involves a total abandonment of the previous condition both socio-economic and familial. On the other hand the discipleship of Jesus shapes itself in its time not as a simple participation in a school, but has such connotations that make of it the participation in a true community of life with Jesus.[16]

This strict association of some to his own specific mission will be more clearly expressed during the discourse of mission found in chapter 10. After having spoken of the concern of Jesus for the harassed and helpless crowd, 'like sheep without a shepherd' (Mt 9:36), the evangelist says that he, 'called to himself his twelve disciples and gave them authority over unclean spirits...'.[17] After the list of these 'twelve apostles', the text says that Jesus sent them, charging them to, 'Go nowhere among the Gentiles, and enter no town of the Samaritans, but go rather to the lost sheep of the House of Israel. And preach as you go saying, "The kingdom of heaven is at hand"' (Mt 10:5–7). In what follows Jesus affirms several times more the identification between himself and these disciples (cf. verses 22, 24ff; and above all verse 40: 'He who receives you receives me').

This strict association between the twelve and the mission of Jesus is stressed once again in chapter 19 verses 27ff: both in the words of Peter, 'Lo, we have left everything and followed you...', and in those of Jesus, 'Truly, I say to you, in the new world, when the Son of man shall sit on his glorious throne, you who have followed me will also sit on twelve thrones, judging the twelve tribes of Israel.' These words are given particular light in the context of chapter 19, in so much as Peter restates the expressions of the radical discipleship which Jesus had proposed to the rich young man, 'Go, sell what you possess and give to the poor, and you will have treasure in heaven; and come, follow me.' (Mt 19:21). We are dealing therefore with a strict association in the mission based on the foundation of a strict community of life, in which, having sold all, one enters and makes oneself a part of the community of Jesus.[18]

One can speak, in fact, of truly being made part of an 'intimacy' of Jesus. From the second part of his gospel, Matthew makes use of the characteristic expression *'kat'idian'* (apart, in his own intimacy). Earlier it was only Jesus who attempted this possibility of being alone with himself and God taking himself to a deserted place apart (Mt 14:13), and then, after having fed the crowd, ascending 'up on the mountain by himself to pray.' (Mt 14:23). Later Jesus 'takes' also the three chosen disciples and took them up the mountain 'apart' (Mt 17:1), for a vision of which they could not speak to anyone 'until the Son of man is raised from the dead.' (Mt 17:9). Eventually Jesus, desiring to predict for the third time his imminent death and resurrection, felt the need to take 'the twelve disciples aside, and on the way he said to them, 'Behold, we are going up to Jerusalem; and the Son of man will be delivered...'' (Mt 20:17)

Jesus desires therefore to open to some, to the twelve, a space of particular intimacy, in which he is able to show more openly the mystery of his person and his destiny. This does not mean that his disciples were deprived of the possibility of being able to approach Him 'apart', of their own accord, in order to have those clarifications that a teacher gives in private to his followers (cf. Mt 17:19 and 24:3).

The particular communion of the twelve is sealed on the Vigil of the Passion, 'when it was evening, he sat at table with the twelve disciples...' (Mt 26:20). And while they were eating he said, 'take [*labete*], eat; this is my body.' And again, 'Drink of it, all of you; for this is my blood of the covenant, which is poured out for many for the forgiveness of sins.' He then added, 'I tell you I shall not drink again of this fruit of the vine until that day when I drink it new with you in my Father's kingdom.' (26:26–29) Jesus thus bonded himself to his twelve disciples with a definitive pact that neither his imminent death nor the scandal of the disciples would be able to break, and that will find its coronation in the kingdom of His Father. Hence, going towards the Mount of Olives he said, 'You will all fall away because of me this night [...]. But after I am raised up, I will go before you to Galilee.' (Mt 26:31–32). And, in fact, in Galilee, on a mountain, Jesus will send the eleven disciples to all the nations.

They were able to find themselves at this meeting with Jesus thanks to those women who were witnesses of His manifestation in the world as true 'Son of God' (Mt 27:54). It seems that we can see here a significant cooperation between 'the women' and 'the brothers' of Jesus in the work of salvation. The mission of 'making disciples' is entrusted to the eleven, but the meeting with the risen Jesus, Lord of heaven and of earth, was possible because the women had the strength and the courage to follow Him until His death on the cross, and they did not leave Him even after His burial. Jesus rewarded this fidelity, giving to the women the mission of reviving in the disciples the memory of His promise. The mission of 'making disciples' is entrusted to the eleven but they have the need of the fidelity of the women that make it through the night.

Do we not see cooperation between a man and a woman also in the generation of Jesus, the Savior? Mary had conceived by the work of the Holy Spirit and had borne a son, but Joseph, the son of David, had to 'take Mary your wife' and give the newborn the name of Jesus, because, 'he will save his people from their sins.' (Mt 1:21). The gift from on high is received first of all by a woman, but this grace has to be accepted alongside the participation of a man in order to be effective in salvation history. Symbolically can we not see this 'cooperation' between the female and male disciples of Jesus refigured in the scene at the burial? Mary of Magdalen and the other Mary contemplated the mystery of the death of Jesus and, in some way, 'received' the Spirit, for this reason they were seated in front of the tomb which for a short time held the body of Jesus. But it was Joseph, the rich man from Arimathea, disciple of Jesus, who having 'took [*labon*] the body' had placed it in a new tomb. The women contemplated the gift of the body of Jesus on the cross, but it is Joseph that physically fulfills the invitation of Jesus, 'Take, this is my body'.[19] Mary and Joseph, at the beginning just as at the end, with different and complementary roles, both of whom are necessary in order that Jesus is able to reach, meet and save all the nations.[20]

Luke

The Lucan work describes the gradual journey of salvation towards Jerusalem (the Gospel) and from Jerusalem (Acts), according to the phrase, '*et videbit omnis caro salutare Dei'* ('every man will see the salvation of God') (Lk 3:6). How is the collaboration between men and women shaped from this perspective?

We will consider here different narratives; first and foremost the virginal conception of Mary. In Luke the virginal birth has numerous dimensions which today have been discussed by various authors.[21] It is noteworthy that from the Old Testament, the relationship between God and His people, and in particular Jerusalem, had been expressed using the spousal metaphor (cf. for example Isaiah 62). This total availability for God and the bond that follows from it finds its highest expression in Mary of Nazareth. 'Rejoice, O full of grace' echoes the words addressed to Sion in Zephaniah 3.

In order to find a place for His presence, God sees once again a city, Nazareth. Here God chooses a space, a place to set down His dwelling, and it had to be a free space, reserved entirely for Him: a young woman in bloom (*'parthenos'*), that did not belong to anybody else (cf. Lk 1:34 'I have no husband'). Here the cloud comes down, here the shadow signals the presence of the most high (cf. Exodus 40). And the son that will be born will be the work of the Holy Spirit, of the creator Spirit. Mary, with a completely personal response, commits herself to the mission that the words of the angel disclose to her: 'Behold, I am the handmaid of the Lord; let it be to me according to your word [*Rema*].'(Lk 1:38). [22]

If the first initiative of God to establish His kingdom takes a man (Zechariah: Lk 1:5–25), it finds its authentic place in Mary, a virginal woman, the handmaid of the Lord: a space and a will open for God (Lk 1:26–38). The comparison between the reactions of Zechariah and Mary shows that if in him there was a hesitating question, in Mary there is only free gift; if Zechariah represents the attitude of the man that reaches out towards God, but does not trust himself entirely to Him, here, in Mary, there is pure acceptance, the availability to the power of God and to His word. If the man questions, the woman knows how to accept.

The visitation of Mary to Elizabeth (Lk 1:39–56) tells of the first expansion of this new presence of God. Two women (Mary and Elizabeth) become the first announcers of the news, the first ones to carry the good news of salvation outside of themselves, with prophetic words, but above all carrying the Lord within.

The story of the birth of Jesus in Bethlehem (Lk 2: 1–20) shows how the presence of the Son of David in the middle of his people receives a double resonance: the first is entrusted by the angels to the shepherds and they, in their turn, tell others; but it is the woman, Mary, who gave birth to her son, who keeps all these things, pondering them in her heart. Against a more external attitude is placed in contrast one that is more interior; both are necessary, but the one is preparatory for the other and from it receives its impetus.

The presentation of Jesus in the Temple (Lk 2:36–38) is also his exposition to all those that went there to worship. He is presented, first of all, to a man, Simeon, and then to a woman: Anna, the prophetess. If Simeon was waiting for the consolation of Israel and God had made him see his salvation, Anna, a virgin before and later a widow, in fasting and in prayer, speaks of Jesus to all that were awaiting the liberation of Jerusalem. The righteous and holy man announces the light, but it is the woman, virgin and praying, that extends it to all.

The resuscitation of the son of the widow of Nain (Lk 7:11–17) shows how the power of the Kingdom of

God, after having reached the servant of a pagan, of the centurion, reaches the son of a widow. The salvation of God is universal and reaches extreme situations: first a man and then a woman. The man intercedes with faith, the woman with tears, but only after the woman was consoled; 'everyone' glorifies God.

The pardon of the sinful woman in the house of Simon the Pharisee (Lk 7:36–50) shows how she experiences the salvation of God because she loved much and she believed. This woman, just like the blind and the sick, extreme categories, experiences the grace of God. But, at the same time, she becomes a model of faith. The mercy of God that is manifested in her has the capacity to open the eyes of others, like, for example, the Pharisee. If the blind simply see and the lame walk, the woman washes, dries, kisses the feet of Jesus. All of her body is active, transformed and thus placed at the service of the gospel of mercy.

The salvation of God reaches a haemorrhaging woman (extreme category), because she demonstrated faith, touching the cloak of Jesus (8:40–48). In a similar way it reached the daughter of Jairus who had also demonstrated faith (8:49–56). The man, the father of the young girl, went to meet Jesus with a prayer, while the woman pressed alongside Him, touching His cloak. But it is the woman who makes the announcement in front of all of the people (cf. v. 47: 'she came trembling, and falling down before him declared in the presence of all the people why she had touched him and how she had been immediately healed.'), while Jesus instructs the parents of the little girl to tell no one what had happened. This represents the dynamic that is referred to at the beginning of chapter 8: Jesus was preaching the Kingdom of God (in words

and works), the twelve were with Him as were some
women who had been healed and provided for Him
out of their means. The contribution of the men seems
to be more towards the generic preaching of the
Kingdom, while the women give testimony in their
flesh to the power of God. The men accompany Jesus,
the women serve Him physically. Men and women are
taken up in the work of salvation and make it known,
but each in their own way.

In Luke 10:38–42 we are presented with the figure
of another Mary, after the mother of Jesus, who, 'sat
at the Lord's feet and listened to His teaching [*logos]*'.
The salvation of God, the knowledge of who is the Son
and of who is the Father (cf. 10:21–22) was given to a
man (the Samaritan) that sees (a victim fallen into the
hands of robbers; cf. v. 10:33) and a woman (Mary,
sister of Martha) that hears. The man comes first, but
it is the woman that captures the full meaning of the
event; it is not enough to do many things, that which
counts is to hear the word of the Lord.

In Luke 11:27–28 to the exclamation of a woman
('Blessed is the womb that bore you and the breasts
that you sucked!') Jesus responds, 'Blessed rather are
those who hear the word of God and keep it!' There is
an evident comparison between the attitude to have
before the word of God and that of a woman towards
her son: first to be welcomed and then nourished.[23]
The woman in the crowd first captures the blessed sign
of the Son of man in her physicality, and thus Jesus is
able to use her expressions to extend the blessing to all
men who hear and put into practice the word of God.
In the same way the Queen of the South, who came
from far away to hear the wisdom of Solomon, ante-
cedes the path of conversion for the men of Nineveh

(cf. vv. 11:29–32): the woman comes first in her perception of salvation indicating its historically determined, concrete character.

Two brief parables illustrate the dynamic character of the Kingdom of God (Lk 13:18–21): it is like a man that threw a grain of mustard into his garden, leaving it to become a tree, and a woman that hides leaven in three measures of flour leaving it to become completely leavened. The man and the woman receive, they are touched by the mystery of the kingdom, but while the attitude of the man is that of throwing it ahead, that of the woman is rather of inserting it into the depths; the two approaches are complementary, but it is the second that reaches the totality.

The discourse on the end of Jerusalem (Lk21:5–36) is preceded by the story of the widow's mite (Lk 21:1–4). The kingdom of God is near — says Jesus in his concluding words (v. 31). One must beware of the things that can weigh us down (v. 34), casting aside all of one's own substance, all of one's own life, into the temple treasury, like the widow. A woman, in an extreme condition, thus becomes the model of the way to embrace salvation, in contrast to the others who gave from their abundance (cf. 21: 4, 35).

In Luke, like in Matthew, the figure of the Virgin Mary at the beginning of the Gospel narrative finds a parallel in the women present in the concluding scene: the passion and resurrection of Christ. After He dies Luke notes, 'And all his acquaintances and the women who had followed him from Galilee stood at a distance and saw these things.' (Lk 23:49) This 'standing', looking at Jesus dying on the cross, recalls the attitude of those women who, while they were leading Jesus to Calvary, 'bewailed and lamented him' (Lk 23:27).

The participation of women in the event of the death of Jesus is expressed here in the silent contemplation of this dramatic spectacle and of the decisive words Jesus pronounced. But after Joseph of Arimathea had taken down the body of Jesus, wrapping it in a linen shroud and placing it in a rock-hewn tomb, 'where no one had ever yet been laid', the women 'saw the tomb, and how his body was laid; then they returned, and prepared spices and ointments.' (Lk 23: 52–56).

Around the king of the Jews that dies, trusting his Spirit to the Father and thus carrying the salvation of his people (23:35–37; 23:39–43), men and women gather. The former carry out practical acts: Simon carries the cross, Joseph places the body in the tomb. Instead, the women have a more affective participation: they bewail, they lament, they contemplate the events and prepare ointments. They anticipate the dynamic of salvation that is conversion and tears and emphasize the point of departure, with the contemplation of the death and tomb of Jesus. Their participation is symbolically expressed by that tomb in which no one had yet been laid and which is found in the text between two mentions of the women of Galilee. Thus, the theme of virginity returns, as a well disposed space, which these people are able to offer for the reception of the presence of God in the world.

Next, on the first day of the week, the women go to the tomb and find it empty. After the angels invited them to 'remember' what Jesus had 'told' them when he was in Galilee, 'they remembered his words, and returning from the tomb they told all this to the eleven...' (Lk 24:8ff). Luke thus seems to strictly link the three stages (death, burial and resurrection) around the figures of the women. The women that followed

Jesus and heard his word, in particular that recalled to them by the angels ('the Son of man must be delivered into the hands of sinful men, and be crucified, and on the third day rise'), now see 'these things', they receive them and protect them as in a virginal womb, of which the new, unused tomb is in some way a symbol. Therefore at the word of the angels, 'they remembered his words' and they announce to the eleven all these things. 'And Peter rose and ran to the tomb'. If the women feel the need to meet with the men concerning their experience, it is also true that the men draw from this communication the strength to pull themselves up and resume their efforts.

To try to summarize, we can say that in the gospel of Luke there is a constant collaboration between men and women shown in different ways. On the one hand the man goes first and the woman deepens (one can think for example of Mary at the annunciation, Mary in labour, to Anna the prophetess, to the widow at Nain, to the sinner, the hemorrhaging woman, to Martha and Mary, to the woman of the leaven); on the other hand the woman goes ahead and demonstrates the right way for the man (one can think for example of the blessed woman and the Queen of the South, to the woman at the Temple Treasury and to the women beside the cross and the tomb):

1. The man pleads, asks, announces, waits, assists, throws the seed; while the woman receives, conserves and meditates, deepens, loves, touches, listens, hides on the inside, but it is through her that salvation becomes universal.

2. The woman is first to intuit the presence of salvation, she is the first to give herself, she

contemplates and converts, she goes to the tomb
and is the first to remember the words of the
Lord. The man then follows the example given
of listening, guarding, detachment, contemplation and conversion.

The man needs the woman so as not to lose his way
through excessive activism; the woman needs the man
in order to have something to think about and learn
from, on which to reflect and deepen, and also to have
a point of reference.

This capacity of the woman to go ahead of the man
in perceiving and announcing salvation seems to have
its foundation specifically in her corporality, her body,
which allows a more immediate contact with the
salvation of God. This is well expressed in the scene of
the visitation.

From this point of view, particular attention seems
to be given to the theme of virginity (one thinks for
example of Mary, Anna and the women at the tomb)
and of widowhood (one thinks again of Anna, the
widow of Nain and the widow at the Treasury). One
can perhaps imagine a particular attention on the part
of God for the poorest, but perhaps also an explicit
space that such people are able to offer to receive the
presence of God in the world.

If in Matthew the theology of the virginity of Mary
had been dominated at Easter by an emphasis which
values the fertile strength of the Spirit, in Luke the
power of the Word of God seems to hold greater value
and dominate. Heard in a virginal space, 'an honest
and good heart' (8:15), the Word of God bears fruit,
leavening all of the earth (cf. 13:20ff).

Mark

The gospel of Mark has a kerygmatic-paradoxical perspective. At the beginning of the gospel, the evangelist presents Jesus as 'Son of God' (Mk 1:1). In fact, the recognition of the truth of this comes only at His death on the cross when the centurion says, 'Truly this man was the Son of God!' (Mk 15:39). In the middle of the gospel, where those around Him question Jesus as to the origin of His wisdom and miracles, an alternative filiation, a more humble origin is proposed, 'Is not this the carpenter, the son of Mary…?' (Mk 6:3). As J. Winandy[24] observes, to identify a man by means of the name of the mother is quite unusual in the Bible. In place of the 'son of the carpenter' (Matthew), Mark simply says, 'the carpenter', but adds, 'son of Mary', thus making a probable allusion to the virginal birth. The typical Marcan dialectic of strength (divine) and weakness (human) thus appears here, Jesus is 'the son of Mary' and exactly because of this is 'the Son of God'. The paradoxical presentation of Jesus as 'son of Mary' prepares for the messianic nature of the cross. Just as Mary, virgin mother, is able to be the place in which God allows His wisdom and power to unfold, so too the women that followed Jesus to the cross are able to be the place that receives the supreme revelation of the 'son of God'. It is not the 'strength' of the man but the 'weakness' of the woman that accords with the messianic nature of the cross.

Starting from this overall vision, we can try to collect the data presented in other pericopes. First of all in the scene of the healing of Peter's mother-in-law (Mk 1:29–34), she is presented as the first image of the true disciple that 'serves them' (cf. Mk 9:35, 'If any one would be first, he must be last of all and servant of all.'; but especially

Mk 10:45, '…the Son of man also came…to serve and to give his life as a ransom for many.').

From another perspective, the resurrection (resuscitation) of the daughter of Jairus (Mk 5:21–43) seems to foreshadow the resurrection of Jesus Himself. Three men (among them James) come to the house of the dead little girl and enter the place where she was; likewise three women (among them Mary, mother of James) come to the tomb of Jesus and enter 'where they had laid Him'. And Jesus said, 'Why do you make a tumult and weep? The child is not dead but sleeping'; At the tomb the young man sitting at the right says, 'Do not be amazed; you seek Jesus of Nazareth…He is risen'; and again, like those present at the resurrection (resuscitation) of the girl who 'were immediately overcome with amazement (*ekstasis*)' so too 'trembling and astonishment' (*ekstasis*) came upon the women (*ekstasis* is used uniquely in these two passages of the gospel of Mark); and finally Jesus strictly charges those at the house of the girl that 'no one should know of this' and of the women it is said that 'they said nothing to anyone'. It is significant that Jesus chooses a small girl of twelve years, a weak being, to announce His victory over the cross.

In this context the figure of the haemorrhaging woman acquires relevance (Mk 5:25–34). She is the embodiment of the faith that saves (that faith that Jesus asks of Jairus, v. 36) a most simple faith, one without words, expressed by the touching of Jesus's garments by this person who is all the more impure.

In the same paradoxical context one can also understand the figure of the Syrophoenician woman, a pagan woman who, despite this, is the first to recognize in Jesus the '*kyrios*', thus opening the Christian mission, beyond Israel, to all the people (Mk 7:24–30). Meanwhile, it is significant that it is the woman's maternal preoccupation, for her daughter's condition , which gives her prophetic acumen.

One can understand in a similar way the choice of the widow as the emblematic figure of one who is poor and despised (Mk 12:41–44) but by giving all of herself (into the treasury 'she out of her poverty has put (*ebalen*) in everything she had, her whole living') realizes the first of the commandments (cf. Mk 12:29), and also the invitation of Jesus that in order to be able to be His disciple, to give 'what you have' (cf. Mk 10:21). Perhaps here also that gift of life is anticipated that Jesus foretold when he said that it is not right to 'throw' (*balein*) the children's bread to the dogs (cf. 7:28).

In the same paradoxical context, one thinks also of the woman of Bethany who anoints the body of Jesus (Mk 14:3–9), participating in anticipation and in such an intimate way in the mystery of His death, the poor person *par excellence*, with the richness that the gift of perfumed ointment represents; and, for this reason, her act is connected to the future proclamation of the gospel (cf. Mk 14:9). The question of those present ('why (*eis ti*) was the ointment thus wasted?') seems to link this act of gift and of death to the death of Jesus; Jesus' words on the cross are evoked, 'why (*eis ti*) hast thou forsaken me?' (These are the only two occurrence of '*eis ti*' in Mark). On the other hand, even under the cross there were bystanders who did not understand the cry of the dying Jesus: 'he is calling Elijah…let us see whether Elijah will come to take him down.'

Finally the women beside the cross, who from afar contemplate his death, are those that fully implement the command of Jesus to follow him, by taking up their own cross. They went up with Him to Jerusalem (cf. Mk 10:32–34), but already they were following Him and serving Him in Galilee. The paradox of the Marcan kerygma concludes with the announcement of the resurrection given to the women; they in their attachment to the body of Jesus (they go to anoint the body, like at Bethany), perhaps even in their weakness and impotence ('who will roll away the stone for us...?') receive the first Easter announcement, that they hold onto in silence, in accordance with the teaching of Jesus.

These figures of women in the gospel of Mark are weak, impure, foreign, despised, but attracted as they are by the person of Jesus and touched by His mercy, they are proposed as figures of the ideal disciple, of the one that follows Jesus up to the cross, thus showing the paradox of the Victory of the Cross, a messianic suffering, which assumes all, transforming human weakness. The power of God, that in them can be shared more effectively, thus values also a series of attitudes, less obvious, but perhaps more suited to the feminine style, such as to serve (a term in Mark that is reserved for the angels, for women and for Jesus), to touch (even if in this gospel it is not used exclusively of women it is predominantly said of them), to anoint, to contemplate ('*theoreo*' is said of the women beside the cross, and at the empty tomb; it is not said of the disciples, but only twice for Jesus and once of demons and of the crowds), to make a total gift of life (the widow). One can think also of a preferential care, although not exclusive, of the body. In fact they are called to a mission of anticipatory and 'fundamental' prophetic witness (cf the Syrophoenician woman and the woman at Bethany), precisely because of their specific attitude. Indeed, without their attention at the cross and their concern for the body of Jesus, without, that is, their mediation ('tell his disciples and Peter that he is going before you to Galilee...') the Christian mystery would have come to nothing.[25]

John[26]

> ... To all who received him, who believed in his name, he gave power to become children of God; who were born, not of blood nor of the will of the flesh nor of the will of man, but of God [of God they were generated (*eghennethesan*)]. (Jn 1:12).

The theme of 'generation' returns at the beginning of the gospel of John, we might say a fecundity of Jesus, to which the end of the gospel also corresponds, 'these are written that you may believe that Jesus is the Christ, the Son of God, and that believing you may have life in His name.' (Jn 20:31). This theme of 'generation' is present also in the conversation that Jesus has with Nicodemus, 'Truly, truly, I say to you, unless one is born anew [or from above], he cannot see the kingdom of God [...] unless one is born of water and the Spirit [...]' (Jn 3:3–5). Here the allusion is to the regenerative death of Christ; cf. 19:30, 34, 'He bowed his head and gave up his spirit [...] but one of the soldiers pierced his side with a spear, and at once there came out blood and water.' Moreover the fecundity of the glorification of the Christ was already predicted in Jn 3:14, 'so must the Son of man be lifted up, that whoever believes in Him may have eternal life.' Later, Jesus says in His prayer, 'I do not pray for these only, but also for those who believe in me through their word.' Also in John therefore, Jesus

strictly associates himself with others in His 'genera-
tive' work. These are His disciples and, first and
foremost, the twelve (Jn 6:70).

It is notable that John also concentrated the attitude
of the ideal disciple in a single figure: 'The disciple that
Jesus loved'. He is the one that during the Last Supper
rested on His chest (Jn 21:20). Jesus desires that he
'remains' with Him until He comes (Jn 21:22). To him
Jesus entrusted His mother and he 'welcomed' her into
his home (Jn 19:26). He is the one that 'saw' and
because of this 'tells the truth—that you may also
believe' (Jn 19:35). And it is this disciple that, on the
first day of the week, runs faster than Peter, reaches
the tomb first, enters after Peter and is first to believe
(Jn 20:4–8); likewise he is first to recognize the risen
Lord on the shores of the lake (Jn 21:7).

It is significant, moreover, that this disciple is fre-
quently also by the side of Peter, in a relationship of
close collaboration. Simon, indicated by Jesus to be the
'rock' (Jn 1:42), makes himself the voice that gathers the
disciples when they are about to abandon Him (Jn 6:68).
It is he that asks the beloved disciple during the Last
Supper of whom He was speaking (Jn 13:24). After
running to the tomb he establishes upon inspection that
it is empty (Jn 20:6). To him Jesus asks a special love
and to him He entrusts his sheep (Jn 21:15–19). His
destiny (to follow Jesus) is significantly juxtaposed to
that of the beloved disciple (to remain until He comes)
(Jn 21:20–23). Thus the relationship of Jesus with those
that he associated with His mission to give 'life' (Jn 10:7)
is not a generic relationship with a group, but has the
characteristic of a personalized relationship, 'preferential' that values the vocations and the ministries of His
disciples in their complementarities.

But also in the fourth gospel between the cross and the resurrection there is a moment of separation, a time in which 'you will be scattered, every man to his home, and will leave me alone' (Jn 16:32). It is the hour when it is 'still dark' (Jn 20:1). At this time, 'standing by the cross of Jesus were his mother, and his mother's sister, Mary the wife of Clopas, and Mary Magdalen' (Jn 19:25). There is here an inclusion with the scene of the first call of the disciples: 'The next day again John was standing with two of his disciples; and he looked at Jesus as he walked and said, "Behold, the Lamb of God!" (Jn 1:35f). The crucified one, beside whom are Mary Magdalen and the others, is in fact the one who fulfils the scripture, 'Not a bone of him shall be broken' (Jn 19:36). And like the two disciples who, having heard the testimony of John, follow Jesus to 'seek' where he lived (cf Jn 1:38), so too Mary Magdalen on the first day of the week, very early in the morning, 'while it was still dark' comes to the tomb 'seeking' Jesus (Jn 20: 1,15). She holds on to the faith that the darkness is not able to overcome the light (cf Jn 1:5). 'You will seek me...' Jesus said (Jn 13:33); but Mary Magdalen is the only one to seek Him in this moment of darkness.

Like he did for the twelve apostles, John concentrated the role and attitude of the women in a single person: Mary Magdalen.[27] Just as the two disciples came and saw where He was living, so Mary Magdalen comes and sees the rock moved away. There follows immediately her run to Peter and the other disciples, which enables an initial upsurge of faith (Jn 20:8). But it will be above all the experience of the encounter with Jesus in the garden and the task received from Him that will allow Mary to go and announce to the disciples, 'I have seen the Lord' and the things He had said to her

(Jn 20:18). In a similar way at the beginning of the gospel, Andrew, having met his brother Simon, had said to him, 'We have found the Messiah' (Jn 1:41). Mary Magdalen had received the fundamental and definitive testimony of Jesus on the cross and alone continued to follow, to seek. She stood weeping outside the tomb. 'You will weep and lament [...] but your sorrow will turn to joy.' (Jn 16:20). The shepherd called her by her name (cf Jn 10:3) and sent her to take the Easter proclamation to His brothers.

Summarizing what we have noted we can thus conclude. The women participate in some way in the regenerating work of humanity above all when they are 'beside' the cross, where Christ gives the Spirit and water ('woman, behold, your son! [...] behold, your mother!'). But it appears still more manifest when Mary Magdalen comes to the disciples announcing, 'I have seen the Lord'; in that moment the disciples faith is regenerated (cf Jn 20:29ff, 'Blessed are those who have not seen and yet believe [...] and that believing you may have life in his name.').

If it is evident that Jesus associates to His mission of salvation, albeit in different ways, in addition to the twelve (and in particular Peter and the beloved), the women (and in particular Mary Magdalen), one can see also how between the two groups there might be cooperation. In particular, without Mary Magdalen, Peter and John would not have been able 'to see' the empty tomb, but it is significant that Mary Magdalen, when confronted by the enigma of the missing body, first and foremost felt the need to turn to the two disciples.

Concluding Reflections

Re-reading the figure of Jesus in the light of the original blessing of Genesis, he appears as the most perfect realization of the image of God.

Jesus Christ is in fact the founder of a new generation in the Spirit, destined to replenish all of the earth: those to whom is given the power to become sons of God. In Him the blessing of Abraham passes to all the nations. The strict bond between the flesh and the promise is broken and it is opened universally. But this fecundity of Jesus is not realized without a strict association of some women with the mystery of redemption, of the regeneration of humanity. They are those that served Him since Galilee, they went up with Him to Jerusalem, they took part in His death and at the tomb they became the first witnesses of His resurrection. Not to mention all those other women that Jesus met during His ministry and that helped Him to show aspects of His salvific mystery. One thinks of the haemorrhaging woman, the Canaanite, the widow's mite, Mary at Cana, and also of the confession of Martha, the sister of Lazarus.

The virginity of Mary is understood within this framework. She inaugurates a condition, an attitude of availability or freedom to the Spirit, to the Word, to the power of God, which will be adopted by other women in a dynamic of reception or welcoming and of maternal fruitfulness. On the other hand this assumption of the woman to Himself in his redemptive work reaches its completion after Easter by vivifying the first and fundamental collaborators of His work: his disciples and especially the twelve. The gospels present them to us as intimately bound to Jesus, constituting an indivisible communion with the master, sharers of His life and His mission. Thus, the concrete action of their mission is strictly connected with the irreplaceable contribution of the women that followed Him from Galilee. Thanks to them the disciples were able to grasp the mystery of Christ in all its depth and breadth.

The celibacy of Jesus is not therefore seen as a renunciation but as a most profound form of realizing the original blessing: a new form of relationship with the woman, in the Spirit, one that enhances her typical nature, with a vision of a universal fecundity. Jesus also introduced His disciples into this new form of fecundity, in a dynamic of exchange and of cooperation in salvation with those women that met Him and that in diverse ways live the virginity of Mary.

Notes

1   This chapter draws, with some modifications and amplifications, on my article 'Il celibato di Gesù e la verginità di Maria' in *Seminarium* 1 (1993), pp. 32–47.

2   M. Orsatti, *Un Saggio di teologia della storia. Esegesi di Mt 1:1–17*, Paideia, Brescia 1980, p. 43.

3   'The end of the Gospel responds to the beginning: thus we have a giant inclusion that demonstrates the universal dimension of the person of Jesus on all of human history...' [J. Radermakers, *Lettura pastorale del vangelo di Matteo*, Bologna 1974, p. 348). Cf Gal 3:14: 'that in Christ Jesus the promise of Abraham might come upon [*genetai*] the Gentiles [*ta ethne*], that we might receive the promise of the Spirit through faith.' Naturally here we are dealing with two very different theological visions (Paul and Matthew), but it is striking that the two frameworks develop the same theme of the offspring of Abraham that, in order to reach all the people, passes through Christ and, as we will see also in Matthew, thanks to the Spirit and to faith.

4   See also X. L. Dufour, 'Livre de la genèse de Jésus Christ' in *Etudes d'Evangile*, Paris 1964, p. 63: 'Selon la chair Jésus est «vierge». Mais, sur un autre plan, sa virginité est féconde. «Venu non pour supprimer, mais pour accomplir», il accomplit la transmission terrestre des bénédictions de Dieu. Désormais, ayant trouvé son terme et son sens en Jésus, l'engendrement sera pleinement spirituel.' See also Mt 1:17c: Jesus is the beginning of the 7th week, in which his genealogy is outlined. With Him the eschatological generation begins.

5   Cf the parable of the mustard seed which immediately precedes (Mt 13:31f).

6   Cf Mt 26:13.

7   Cf Mt 15:21–28.

8   Cf Mt 9:18ff.

9   Cf Mt 26:56.

10   Cf X. L. Dufour, 'L'annonce à Joseph' in *Etudes d'Evangile*, Paris 1964, p. 76.

11   This specification is not found in Mark but is in Luke.

12   It ought to be noted that for all four gospels the tomb is first
     of all *'mnemeion'*.

13   Cf Mt 27:51ff '...the rocks *were split;* the tombs also *were
     opened,* and many bodies of the saints who had fallen asleep
     were raised, and *coming out of* the tombs after his resurrection.

14   Cf Mt 25:1ff.

15   Cf Mt 24:38.

16   Cf J. M. Lozano, *La Sequela di Cristo,* Milano 1981, pp. 17–31.

17   On the typical but also historical role of the 'twelve disciples'
     in Matthew, cf. in particular U. Luz, 'Die Junger im
     Matthausevangelium' *in ZNW* 62 (1971), pp. 141–171; S.
     Legasse, 'Il vangelo secondo Matteo' in Aa. Vv., *Il ministero e
     i ministeri secondo il NT,* Roma 1979, pp. 269ff.

18   In this same chapter 19 is also found the noteworthy verse 12
     ('For there are eunuchs who have been so since birth, and there
     are eunuchs who have been made eunuchs by men, and there
     are eunuchs who have made themselves eunuchs for the sake
     of the kingdom of heaven.') For related discussions and for its
     value in documenting the celibate state of Jesus, see J. Blinzler,
     'eisin eunuchoi. Zur Auslegung von Mt. 19:12' *in ZNW* 48 (1957),
     pp. 254–270; cf also my article 'Il Celibato nel NT' in *La Scuola
     Cattolica* 110 (1982), pp. 333–370, subsequently reproduced i n
     my book *Celibato sacerdotale e celibato di Gesu,* Piemme, Casale
     Monferrato 1987.

19   Cf Gregory of Nazianzus, *Oratio* 45, 23–24 in *PG* 36, 654: 'Si
     Joseph Arimataeus sis, ab eo, qui cruci affixit, corpus pete;
     tuum fiat mundi piaculum.'

20   We do not intend here to constrict the contribution of women
     and of men in the work of salvation to rigidly determined
     roles, but only to show how the mystery of Christ is transmit-
     ted to the world with the joint contribution of both according
     to specific and complementary modes.

21   See especially the study of I. De La Potterie, 'La Vergine
     Maria' in *La verginità cristiana,* Parola Spirito e Vita 1980, pp.
     95–114.

22   *'Rema'* is a Semitic word which reflects the double meaning
     of *'dabar"* (*'word',* *'thing'*). Later it will be said twice that Mary,
     'kept all these things [*remata*]' (Lk 2: 19, 51).

23   Cf also 8:21, 'My mother and my brothers are those who hear the word of God and do it.'

24   J. Winandy, 'La conception virginale dans le N.T.' in *NRT* 100 (1978), 707ff.

25   In this regard, see also C. Ricci, *Maria di Magdala e le molte altre. Donne sul cammino di Gesu*, D'Auria, Napoli, 1991.

26   The original contribution of the fourth gospel will be presented more fully in the second chapter. Here only certain elements are offered, that address the themes already found in the Synoptic Gospels.

27   Mary Magdalen also had a prominent role in the Synoptic Gospels.

2

The Mother of Jesus and the Gathering of the Scattered

N THE GOSPEL of John the salvific work of Christ completed on the cross is presented as the gathering of the scattered, the lost, the dispersed, the unification of men.[1] In this work, what role is assigned to the mother of Jesus, who stood 'by the cross' and to whom Jesus says, 'Woman behold your son'? In order to respond to this question we will need to examine, beyond the episode on the cross (Jn 19:25–27), also that episode which corresponds to it from the beginning of the fourth gospel: the wedding at Cana (2:1–12). Departing from this general framework, we will see how the relational dynamic between Jesus and Mary, the 'woman', meanders and develops in the course of the Gospel of John in other episodes (the Samaritan woman at the well; Martha, Mary and Lazarus; the anointing at Bethany) that will help to better specify the meaning of the mission of the mother of Jesus in the work of gathering the scattered.

Mary at the foot of the Cross (John 19:25–27)

The scene of the dialogue between Jesus on the cross and His mother is located in the third section of the passion according to John (Jn 19:23–42).[2] This section comprises 5 episodes structured as follows:

A: 23–24: The soldiers (fulfilment of Scripture)

B: 25–27: The disciples

C: 28–30: Jesus: 'It is finished' (because Scripture is fulfilled)

A': 31–37: The soldiers (fulfilment of Scripture)

B': 38–42: The disciples[3]

Jesus (in the centre), true paschal lamb, dies, giving his Spirit, and thus gives fulfilment to the Scriptures and to his work in the act of definitive love (cf. Jn 13:1). 'Jesus, knowing that all was now finished said (to fulfil Scripture), 'I thirst.' […] When he had received the vinegar, he said, "It is finished"' (Jn 19:28–30).

This fulfilment is seen on the one hand in the first and in the fourth scene when, in the fact that the soldiers do not tear the clothing or break the legs of Jesus but pierce His side, John brings out a more profound meaning. Christ, raised from the earth, draws all to Himself in faith and proposes Himself as the new temple, the temple of the eschatological gathering from whose right side flows the water that springs for eternal life. On the other hand, Jesus, with His death on the cross is strength against every lacerating tendency. In their decision, taken 'by the cross', not to tear the clothing of Jesus, the soldiers are unaware executors of a divine plan announced in psalm 21 that has its realization in the death of Christ. The clothing is not torn because the permanent foundation of the unity of believers is the unity between Jesus and the Father, revealed on the cross. The clothing is not torn because it is the flock of Jesus, only one shepherd, who is one with the Father and no one will be able to snatch His sheep from His hand (cf. also Jn 21:11: 'and although there were so many, the net was not torn').

On the other hand it seems that the fulfilment of the Scriptures and of the work of Jesus ought to be read also in the faithful rush of some disciples, who *receive* the body in order to take care of it; and in the gesture of Jesus, who indicates the son to the mother and she is *received* him. The disciple, first fruit and sign of all those that are and will be gathered by the glory of the Lord, 'welcomes' the woman into his home (intimacy): the woman who is at the same time the mother of Jesus, united to Him in the work of regeneration of the faith of men, and also the figure of the new city of those saved by the Lord from the dispersion, namely of the new Jerusalem.[4]

We cannot ignore that in this scene the old prophecy of Jerusalem is in some way fulfilled: the mother who sees her scattered sons return to her, gathered by the power of the Lord.[5] We must remember also that Jerusalem would become the centre of the pilgrimage of the people, exactly because of the glory of the Lord, who would be raised above her. Now Jesus had said, 'The hour has come for the Son of man to be glorified [...] and I, when I am lifted up from the earth, will draw all men to myself.' (Jn 12: 23, 32). Jesus, raised up on the cross, makes shine forth the glory of God and those that believe gather themselves in his light (cf. the actions of Joseph of Arimathea and Nicodemus).

As A. Kerrigan notes,[6] in Isaiah God, after having turned to Jerusalem and having indicated that the sons return to her, he then turns to the same sons (Is 50:1–3; 66: 5ff), speaking to them of their mother. We see the same happen at Calvary: Jesus now reveals and gives the mother to the disciple[7]. The work of the gathering of the Servant of YHWH has reached its conclusion, the sons are again gathered around their mother. In some way the scene rises to a summary representation of the reason Jesus came, the purpose of His life's work about to be completed definitively with His death: the new convocation of the scattered people from the dispersion. After Jesus added, turning to the disciple, 'behold your son!' it is said, 'And from that hour the disciple took her to his own home.' He opens himself, opens his home (intimacy) to the mother of Jesus, his availability for communion with Jesus, with the Word, and so all that he began and fulfilled in the world is perfected.[8] To welcome Mary signifies to welcome Christ, especially in so much as it fulfils His work of the reunification of men.[9]

Mary at Cana (Jn 2:1–13)

As noted all of the fourth gospel is enclosed in a great 'inclusion' by two episodes that represent the mother of Jesus (2:1–13 and 19:25–27) and in which Jesus turns himself to her with the name 'woman'.[10] In order to better understand the scene at the foot of the cross, it is also necessary to consider the marriage at Cana.

John places the miracle at Cana in relation with the revelation of Sinai (Ex 19:16) and with that of the Easter mystery: all three events are dated on the third day. Just as on Sinai God manifested his glory and gave the law, here Jesus manifests His glory, giving new wine, symbol of the new law. Just as on Sinai the manifestation of God came after all the people had declared themselves available for God ('All that the Lord has spoken we will do' Ex 19:8), here at Cana Jesus gives His first sign after His mother said, 'Do whatever he tells you.' If the community of Israel was often presented under the image of a 'woman', here Jesus challenges His mother exactly thus, 'O woman, what have you to do with me? My hour has not yet come.' (Jn 2:4). And it is exactly the openness of the mother to the will of the Son that prepares the conditions so that the sign of the glory of the Messiah is performed. This manifestation kindles the disciples' faith in Jesus and they go down to Capernaum united to Him, to His mother and brothers.[11]

Here the dynamic, realized by faith, of unification around Christ is emphasized. It is a dynamic already apparent in Jn 1:35–51, where the progressive revelation of the transcendent identity of Jesus provoked a series of disciples to gravitate towards Him in succession. This dynamic is present throughout the fourth gospel and is expressed most clearly in Jn 17:20–22 ("I do not pray for these only, but also for those who believe in me[…] that they may be one even as we are one").[12] The celebration of the covenant with God, the hearing of the Word unifies the community of believers,[13] but also in the episode at Cana we see clearly the interaction between the Christ and His mother that characterizes this process of salvation. It is the mother who opens the way, who triggers the events that will lead to the manifestation of the glory, to the faith in Jesus, to the convergence of believers towards Him.

Without the intervention of Mary, representative of the people of Israel in its poverty ('they have no wine')[14] and her openness to the Word of God and of His messenger,[15] the better wine would not have been offered to humanity. Through the intercession of Mary, the glory of Jesus was manifested; heard and interiorized in faith it became an inebriating experience for His disciples, the first of the signs, a first realization of the unity of the scattered.[16] In this episode the role of Mary beside the cross is foreshadowed; her adhesion to the will of the Son, decisive for the completion of the sign, finds its highest expression in the 'standing by the cross' exactly where Jesus reveals her role to her: 'Woman, behold, your Son!'

The Samaritan Woman (Jn 4:4–42)

From what we have said so far, we can see how the role of Mary in the work of gathering the scattered can be strictly linked to her condition as 'woman'. It seems useful also to take into consideration the episode of the Samaritan woman. In fact, in the story of the encounter between Jesus and the Samaritan woman (Jn 4:4–42) we see once again a woman with a determinant role in the dynamic of salvation: to inspire a 'coming to' Jesus in faith.[17]

The episode has two stages: vv. 4–26 and vv 27–42. In the first part the appearance on the scene of a woman from Samaria provokes Jesus to a series of declarations, that progressively reveal his own particular identity: he is a Jew (v. 9), but he is greater than Jacob (v. 12) because he is able to give the living water that wells up to eternal life (v. 14); he is a prophet (v. 19), even better he is the Messiah (v. 26), who announces a new cult of God in Spirit and Truth. In the second part the coming to the faith of the Samaritans is described, provoked by the word of the woman moved by her encounter with Jesus. But this central movement has an even more profound meaning revealed by the words of Jesus Himself to His disciples (vv. 31–38): the Samaritans that are coming (v. 30), and that soon will believe in Him (v. 41) are for Jesus the first of the messianic harvest; with them the eschatological gathering predicted by the prophets begins to be realized. 'Raise your eyes and look': in the Old Testament this is an invitation to contemplate the greatness of God and in particular the re-unification of the scattered of Israel and of all the nations (Is 29:18; 60:4; Bar 5:5–6).[18] This is the work of the Father, 'of Him who sent me', that Christ wishes to complete (v. 34): this is His food. Speaking with the woman at the Well of Sychar, notwithstanding the surprise and the prejudices of the disciples, Jesus was doing the will of the Father and trying to complete His work.

It is evident how the role of the woman is pivotal in this salvific event (cf. v. 42: 'this is indeed the Saviour of the world'). It is her that first and foremost moves herself towards the source of the living water, thus she inaugurates and prefigures the way for her fellow citizens (cf. verse 7: 'There came a woman of Samaria to draw water', with verse 30: 'They […] were coming to him'). Then there are the two questions of the woman, somewhere between the naïve and the embarrassed but always linked to her concrete lived experience, that provoke the manifestation of Jesus as the Messiah. And finally it is her persistent testimony that leads to her fellow citizens believing and going towards Jesus, the first of the eschatological harvest, the gathering of the scattered (vv. 39ff). Mary Magdalen will have a similar anticipatory, explorative role 'the first day of the week'. She also 'came to the tomb' (Jn 20:1) and then goes to the disciples to tell them what she saw. And, 'Peter then came out with the other disciple and they went toward the tomb': and finally the other disciple went in and 'saw and believed' (Jn 20:8). This sequence is to be compared to Jn 4:7: 'There came a woman from Samaria to draw water', and then, after the provocation of Jesus, the woman went into the city to tell the men all that had happened to her; 'they went out of the city and were coming to him', 'and from that city many believed in him' (Jn. 4:39).

Martha and Mary (Jn 11)

The book of signs, the first part of the fourth gospel, opens with the Miracle of Cana in which the intercession of a woman has great importance. It is thus appropriate that this first part of the gospel concludes with an even more clamorous sign, the resurrection of a dead man by Jesus, prompted by the intercession of another two women: Mary and Martha.

As Jesus' hour approaches there is a gradual intensification of the motifs of death and resurrection (Jn 11: 1–44) leading to the climax of the decisive reaction on the part of the Sanhedrin (vv. 45–47). The masterly dramatic composition that characterizes this pericope (belonging, like chapter 12 to which it is strictly united, to a later redaction), after the appeal of the sisters to Jesus, in turn brings to our attention his playing for time and the risky nature of the mission (1–16), then the figure of Martha (17–27), and that of Mary (28–37); then we reach the moment of the resurrection of

Lazarus. To this sign is attributed the faith of many (v. 45) and the decision of the Sanhedrin to put to death 'one man', so that all the nation should not perish, but also, as the evangelist stresses, 'to gather into one the children of God who are scattered abroad.' (v. 52)

This event, in which Jesus, going to die for his friend, is revealed as the resurrection and the life not only for His people but for all the sons of God, is clearly brought about through the intercession of two women. Their faith in Jesus is determinant for the manifestation of His glory. The central verse, 11:27, places on the lips of Martha the most complete Christological profession of the fourth gospel: 'You are the Christ, the Son of God, he who is coming into the world.' This profession is framed by vv. 21 and 32 in which it is affirmed, 'Lord, if you had been here, my brother would not have died.' Thus the declaration of Jesus is anticipated, 'I am the resurrection and the life; he who believes in me, though he die, yet shall he live [...]' (vv. 25f). It is appropriate to note also that Mary, when she hears said: 'The teacher is here and he is calling you (*fonei*)' rose (*egerthe*) quickly and went to Him (v. 29), thus anticipating the scene of the resurrection of Lazarus, who comes out upon hearing the powerful voice (*fone*) of Jesus who was calling him (vv. 43f).

The resurrection of Lazarus is the first consequence of the faithful appeal of Mary and Martha. It has all the characteristics of an anticipation of the resurrection of Jesus;[19] but it deals only with an anticipatory sign of the salvation that Jesus brings. The appeal of the two women though also prompts another effect, the decision of the Sanhedrin to put Jesus to death so that the whole nation should not perish and thus he will be able to 'gather into one the children of God who are scattered abroad.'

The faith of the two women accelerates the dramatic fulfillment of the events of salvation. They draw Jesus towards the field of His adversaries (v.8), they provoke the revelation of His glory (v.40) and they trigger that dynamic of faith (v.45) that with Easter will reach universal horizons (v.52)[20]. Another significant aspect is the role of the point of convergence for those that believe in Jesus played by Martha and above all by Mary. The central section presents an inclusion between v. 19 ('many of the Jews had come to Martha and Mary to console them concerning their brother') and v. 45 ('Many of the Jews therefore, who had come with Mary and had seen what he did, believed in him'). The section dedicated to the figure of Mary notes that when she raises herself in order to go to Jesus who calls, 'the Jews who were with her in the house [...] saw Mary rise quickly and go out, they followed her [...]' (v.31). And a little later Jesus sees Mary 'weeping and the Jews who came with her also weeping' (v.33). Mary, the woman who is docile to the word of Jesus and has faith in Him, already forms a point of gathering of those that 'came towards her' almost as preparation for the convergence of those that 'believed in Jesus'.[21]

Mary and the Anointing of Bethany (Jn 12:1–11)

The event of the resurrection of Lazarus continues to have consequences in the gospel of John. Chapter 12 illustrates the development, presenting the theme of the regal nature of Jesus and thus anticipating the mystery of His passion. Except for the final part (vv36b-50, a first assessment of the salvific work of Jesus) the chapter is divided into two parts: 1–19 and 20–36a.

The first part stresses above all the theme of Jesus, King of Israel (v.13), while the second emphasizes the universal character of his lordship (cf. v. 32: 'I... will draw all men to myself'). Verses 12:1–19 are divided into two parallel scenes:[22] verses 1–11: the anointing as presaging of death; verses 12–19: royal entrance as anticipation of glorification.[23]

The anointing done by Mary at Bethany (Jn 12:1–11) may well have a regal character.[24] In any event, with her prophetic gesture, Mary indicates the inestimable, superabundant worth of the imminent death of Jesus, whose perfume of life (12,3) contrasts with the odour of death of the tomb of Lazarus (v. 11, 39). The critical intervention of Judas (Why was this ointment not sold for three hundred denarii and given to the poor?'), precisely because of its reasonableness in the male mould, stresses the contrast with the feminine logic of superabundance and gratuity. This paradox follows that of the parallel episode at the marriage at Cana: there also, the steward of the feast emphasizes how in general the good wine is served at the beginning and 'when the men have drunk freely, then the poor wine'. The intervention of the mother of Jesus meant that the good wine was instead reserved to the end.[25] Here the logic of superabundance that characterizes all of the ministry of Jesus is reflected: 'The thief comes only to steal [...] I came that they may have life and have it abundantly' (Jn 10:10; cf 6:12ff).[26]

The section concludes, as does the sign of the resurrection of Lazarus, with the mention of the multitude that come in order to see Jesus and Lazarus and believe in Him (vv. 9–11). The dynamic of the

manifestation of the mystery of Jesus continues, anticipated in that of the death and resurrection of Lazarus,
that is also a movement of convergence to Him in faith
(cf. 11:51 ff: 'Jesus should die [...]to gather into one the
children of God who are scattered abroad.').

The following question emerges: what is the role of
Mary in this salvific dynamic? In this context we need
to stress above all the parallelism between this scene
and the following one, the washing of the feet (ch. 13).
In addition to the global significance of the banquet
(*deipnon:* 12:2, cf 13:2), the following parallels are
noted: v. 12:1: 'Six days before Passover'; v. 13:1:
'Before the feast of Passover when Jesus knew...'; v.
12:3 'Mary took a pound of costly ointment [...]
anointed the feet of Jesus and wiped his feet with her
hair'; cf. 13:4ff '[Jesus] girded himself with a towel [...]
and began to wash the disciples' feet, and to wipe them
with a towel'; v. 12:4: 'But Judas Iscariot, one of his
disciples (he who was about to betray him) said...'; cf
v. 13:2: 'And during supper, when the devil had
already put it into the heart of Judas Iscariot, Simon's
son, to betray him.'

Beyond this analogy of context and symbolic gestures,
the reactions that follow reveal a parallelism. Judas
demonstrates incomprehension of the act of Mary, just
as Peter will do concerning the act of Jesus. And as Jesus
does not agree with the criticism made by Judas, neither
does he share the reaction of Peter. Positively, Jesus
indicates instead the meaning of the act of Mary in
relation to His upcoming burial,[27] likewise He says to
Peter that he will understand the meaning of his act
'afterward', alluding again to His salvific death, when
from His side will flow 'blood and water'.[28]

Mary thus anticipates the prophetic act of Jesus in its dimensions of humble, fraternal service, but also together foreshadowing His death and resurrection for the salvation of the world. His death, evoked here, will be a perfume that will fill the entire house; the Pharisees comment at the end of the next scene, 'Look, the world has gone after him' (Jn 12:19). One may say that Jesus learns from Mary of Bethany the logic of the gratuitous, superabundant gift, just as he had learnt from Mary His mother at Cana. The act of Mary anticipates that of Jesus, it is an example, a model, it opens a way, but at the same time it depends on it; in the sense that Mary, like Martha, acts from the position of faith in the teacher that resuscitated her brother (12:1). Mary intuits the greatness of the mystery of Jesus and with her curious act manifests its extraordinary nature.

The next scene, the triumphant entry into Jerusalem, (vv. 12–19) amplifies the preceding ideas. Jesus is presented as the king of Israel (v. 13) and 'a great crowd' go to meet Him and acclaim Him (vv. 12ff): 'Look, the world has gone after him' is the final comment (v. 19), that introduces the scene that follows: the approach of the Greeks and the declaration of Jesus: 'I, when I am lifted up from the earth, will draw all men to myself' (12:32). The entire universe (*ho kosmos*) finds its unity, its order, in the faith of Jesus, its king and its judge,[29] obedient to the Father, raised up on the Cross.

If this is the salvific mystery of Jesus, it is evident that Mary of Bethany had a role that anticipates its substance with an act of high symbolic value: an anointing that had filled the entire house with its perfume.

Concluding Reflections

'Woman, behold your son', 'behold your mother'. These words which echo those of the ancient prophets on the pilgrimage to Zion of all the people of the world, are also the indication for Mary of a role that is fulfilled and begins again at the same time. Such a role is gradually illustrated by the evangelist from a starting point in chapter 2. As we have in fact seen, the figure of the 'woman' in the fourth gospel, beginning in the episode of the wedding at Cana, then with the scene of the Samaritan woman, and then the figures of Mary and Martha, right up until the death of Jesus on the cross, has a determinant role in the dynamic of salvation.

If in Cana the mother of Jesus, prompting the Son to the first manifestation of His glory, triggered the first movement of the gathering of the believers around Jesus, no less fundamental was the role of the Samaritan woman in bringing closer to the Savior of the world the first fruits of the eschatological harvest, her fellow citizens who believed in Him through her word; while on the other hand she anticipated this movement of faith by going first to draw at the spring that wells for life everlasting.

To these two feminine figures at the beginning of the 'book of signs' are two corresponding figures at the end of this part of the gospel: Martha and Mary. These two also have the role of accelerating the completion of the events of salvation, prompting Jesus to manifest his glory, thus triggering the movement of faith that will make all converge towards Jesus. Moreover, Mary and Martha also precede in faith their fellow citizens, in so much as they are the first ones on the path to Jesus, proclaiming their faith in Him, who is the resurrection and the life, the Son of God who has to come into the world. Finally, as the mother of Jesus had opened the way to the extraordinary gift of her Son in her concern for the lack of wine, so Mary of Bethany opened the way with her perfumed oil to the washing of the disciples' feet by Jesus.

Therefore there is a frame, a 'clasp'[30], of these four episodes with feminine protagonists that contains the entire book of signs (chapters 1 to 12) with a concentric correspondence:

A) 2:1–12: Mary at Cana

B) 4:1–42: the Samaritan Woman

B') 11:1–52: Martha and Mary

A') 12:1–11: Mary and the Anointing at Bethany

Beyond the concentric parallelism (ch 2//ch 12 and ch 4//ch 11), there is also need to bring to attention that between chapter 2 and chapter 11: the woman signals an emerging need, that initially is not recognized (indeed, there had been a certain holding of it at a distance), but then is taken into consideration and becomes a determining stage in the itinerary of Jesus (first sign, seventh sign that opens the door to death).

In conclusion, all the ministry of Jesus, from the first of the signs, that at Cana, until the seventh sign, that at Bethany (12:18), receive impulse and light from the presence of the woman, thus preparing the concluding scene of the mother of Jesus under the cross.

Wishing to schematize the characteristics of these feminine appearances in the frame of the events of salvation, one would be able to say that there is a function of both provocation and anticipation on the part of the woman. If on the one hand she prompts, pushes and helps Jesus to manifest His glory (as at

Cana, the well of Sychar and at Bethany); on the other
hand she anticipates that total gift of self that is the
nucleus of the paschal mystery of Jesus (as at Cana and
in the banquet of Bethany). Not only, but also the
woman is the first to place herself on a path of faith
that others will later go down, prototype of the messianic community at Cana, forerunner of the city of the
Samaritans, first fruit of the Jews of Jerusalem that
believe in Jesus.[31]

At the same time, we need to note that this participation of women in the work of salvation is, on two
occasions, placed on a different level to that of a more
rational male approach. While in general the signs of
Jesus come to meet a primary, urgent need (illness,
hunger, blindness), the intervention of the two women
at Cana and at Bethany point to the superfluous, the
gratuitous, the symbolic. One may say that the woman
has here a prophetic role of anticipating in evocative
and poignant symbols the sweetness and fragrance of
the salvation brought by Jesus.

Moreover it is twice stressed (both at the wedding
at Cana, and before the illness of Lazarus) that the
intervention of the woman comes like an element of
'disturbance' in the planning of Jesus, pushing Him,
after an initial hesitation, to change program; but it is
exactly from this rupture that new life is born.

It is appropriate therefore that Jesus from the cross
says to his mother, calling her with the generic address
'woman', 'behold your son'. That disciple who Jesus
loved and who represents all believers, the sons of God
gathered by Christ beside His cross, drawn by His
glory, was in fact generated also by her, by the
'woman', who provoked and anticipated the gift of His
life, that life in superabundance that Jesus came to

give.[32] With her intervention of total trust in her Son at Cana, Mary anticipated in the sign of the wine the manifestation of the hour of Jesus; with her presence 'beside the cross' she takes a living part in the reality of the full manifestation of the glory of the Son. The evangelist distinguishes well the situation of the four women, who were 'standing by the cross of Jesus', from that of the disciple, who was 'standing near' the mother of Jesus. The situation of the mother of Jesus and the other three women thus assumes a summary presentation of the role of the woman in the work of Christ, not in the sense of a 'double feminine', but in the sense of an original co-participation which is exactly what is delineated in the course of the narrative; co-participation that moves Jesus to designate Mary as the mother of the beloved disciple; and dealing precisely of a co-participation, Jesus cannot help but point out that the gathering of the dispersed sons of God, that He had to realize, attracting all to Himself, is completed in fact also around His mother.[33] In fact if the Prologue speaks of the necessity of accepting Jesus in order to become sons of God, here the disciple accepts into his intimacy the mother of Jesus.[34] The connection that associates Jesus and the 'woman' could not be expressed in a more profound way.

This maternal function of the mother of Jesus, of the 'woman', naturally does not conclude at the cross, but is permanent, as the figure of Mary Magdalen illustrates well at sunrise on the first day of the week, when, preceding all, she discovers the empty tomb and with her announcement gives back life to the disciples.

If the events now evidenced help to understand the relationship between Jesus and the woman in the mystery of salvation, they are also able to illuminate in general the relationship between man and woman. In this regard it ought to be noted how in the fourth gospel, which develops further and deepens the relationship between Jesus and the 'woman', there is no trace of a spousal relationship between Jesus and a woman. This means to say that a meaningful relationship between a man and a woman is possible beyond that of the spousal relationship and that moreover this relationship has its own specific open and universal fecundity. The result of this co-operation is not 'a son', but 'the sons of God' gathered in unity.

Notes

1   Cf John 11:52; 17:22–23; for a broader consideration of this theme see D. Marzotto, *L'unità degli uomini nel vangelo di Giovanni*, Paideia, Brescia 1977.

2   For this structure see chapter 7 of the work cited above in which is also found a related discussion.

3   Cf. Marzotto, *L'unità degli uomini nel vangelo di Giovanni*, p. 203.

4   Cf. *Ibid.*, p. 213.

5   Cf Is 49: 20; 60:4–7; Bar 4:30 ff; Ps 11:2ff; see also Jer 10:17; cf A. Kerrigan, 'Jn 19:25–27 in the light of Johannine Theology and the Old Testament' in *Antonianum* 35 (1960), pp. 369–416.

6   *Ibid.*, p. 410.

7   Cf, M. De Goedt, 'Un scheme de révélation dans le quatrième Evangile' in *NTS* 8 (1961–62), p. 150.

8   Cf. I. De La Potterie, 'La maternità spirituale di Maria e la fondazione della Chiesa (Jn 19:25–27)' in *Gesù Verità*, Marietti, Torino 1973, p. 163.

9   Cf. Marzotto, *L'unità degli uomini nel vangelo di Giovanni*, pp. 209ff; on this section see also the fundamental work of A. Serra, *Contributi dell'antica letteratura giudaica per l'esegesi di Giovanni, 2, 1–12 e 19,25–27*, Herder, Roma 1977.

10 On this point see Serra, *Contributi dell'antica letteratura giudaica per l'esegesi di Giovanni, 2,1–12 e 19, 25–27*.

11 Cf. A. Serra, *Maria a Cana e presso la croce. Saggio di Mariologia giovannea (Gv 2, 1–12 e 19, 25–27)*, Roma 1978, p. 71.

12 Cf. 2:23; 4:39; 6:2; 7:31; 8:30; 10:42; 11:45; 12:11; 12:42; 19:23–42; 21:11. On this point see Marzotto, *L'unità degli uomini nel vangelo di Giovanni*, p. 238.

13 On this point see D. Marzotto, 'Giovanni 17 e il Targum di Esodo 19–20' in *Riv Bibl It* 25 (1977), pp. 375–388

14 Cf. X. Leon-Dufour, *Lecture de l'evangile selon Jean*, vol. I, Du Seuil, Paris 1988, p. 226.

15 *Ibid.*, p. 235.

16 On this aspect, also very suggestive are the writings of M. Garzonio, *Gesù e le donne*, Rizzoli, Milano 1990, ch. 1–2

17 According to F. Moloney, *The Gospel of John*, Collegeville, Minnesota 1998, p. 64 and p. 114, in the section 2:1–4:54 (from cana to Cana) the two reactions to the words of Jesus (of the Jews and the non-Jews) are presented. In this structure the two female figures would constitute an evident parallelism. Of this, what is immediately apparent are certain terminological correspondences ('woman': 2:4, 4:7; 'draw water' 2:8, 4:7).

18 Cf. Marzotto, *L'unità degli uomini nel vangelo di Giovanni*, pp. 153ff.

19 Certain parallels can be seen: 'tomb' (*mnemeion*): 11:38 and 20:1; 'where they have laid him': 11:34 and 20:2; 'Take away the stone': 11:39 and 20:1; 'cloth'/'napkin'/'shroud' (*soudarion* translations differ) 11:44 and 20:7.

20 Cf. Marzotto, *L'unità degli uomini nel vangelo di Giovanni*, pp. 131–140.

21 It is notable how in the fourth gospel the movement of those that 'come towards' Jesus (*erchomai pros auton*) is propaedeutic and even equivalent to 'believe in Him' (*pisteuo eis auton*) (cf. ad esempio 6:35; 10:41).

22 The recurrence at the beginning and the end (vv.1 and 17) of the resurrection of Lazarus gives unity to the whole of these two scenes.

23   For an analogous parallelism see Jn. 2:1–12 and 13–22; where
     the sign of the wine (presaging of the hour of the passion) is
     placed alongside the sign of the temple (pre-annunciation of
     the resurrection); see also the recurrence of the information
     that the disciples 'remembered' after His glorification (2:22
     and 12:16).

24   Cf A. Lion, *Lire saint Jean*, Paris, Cerf 1972, p. 87.

25   See Jn 2:10, 'you have kept (*teterekas*) the good wine until
     now'; cf 12:7 'Let her keep (*terese*) it for the day of my burial'.

26   Judas instead is characterized as a 'thief' (*kleptes:* 12:6).

27   On the difficulties of the translation of 12:7, cf. Moloney, *The
     Gospel of John*, pp. 349–357; he proposes the following trans-
     lation, 'the purpose was that she might keep this for the day
     of preparation for my burial'

28   These parallelisms are highlighted also by P. Mourlon Beer-
     naert, *Marthe, Marie et les autres. Les Visages feminins de
     l'Evangile*, Lumen vitae, Bruxelles 1992, p. 1667; see also R.
     Fabris, *Giovanni*, Borla, Roma 1992, p. 675; Y. Simoens, *Selon
     S. Jean*, IET, Bruxelles 1997, p. 470.

29   Cf. '*seated on the colt of a donkey*' (12:15) e 19:13: 'Pilate ...
     brought Jesus out and sat down on the judgment seat'. For
     this interpretation, see I. De La Potterie, 'Gesù re e giudice
     secondo Giovanni 19:3' in *Gesù Verità*, Marietti, Torino 1973,
     pp. 134–157, even if not everyone shares this position (cf.
     Moloney, *The Gospel of John*, p. 500).

30   To use the expression of A. Feuillet, in Italian the expression
     is *fibbia*.

31   We cannot say the same for Nicodemus or for the man born
     blind since, in their respective episodes, a subsequent move-
     ment of faith of others is not recorded.

32   CF. M. Gourgues, 'Marie 'la femme' et la 'mère' en Jean' in
     NRT 108 (1986), pp. 174–191

33   As will be recalled, Mary of Bethany provided a shadowing
     of such a role as point of convergence regarding the Jews who
     were to believe in Jesus.

34   On this point see I. De La Potterie, *Maria nel mistero dell'alleanza*,
     Marietti, Genova 1988, pp. 243f.

3

FIGURES OF WOMEN IN THE ACTS OF THE APOSTLES

OR SOME TIME scholars have highlighted the significant presence of female figures in the Acts of the Apostles.[1] In particular, M. Perroni proposes the thesis according to which the participation of women in the Christian mission and in the ecclesial life of the first generation is detectable in a conspicuous way in the Acts, while in the gospel of Luke there is a 'marked asymmetry' between men and women, a marginalization of the women. In his eyes, Luke would have found traditions of a conspicuous presence of the woman in the Church, which he would have then progressively scaled, both in the Acts, and in particular in the gospel, in view of his ecclesiology.[2] In general the studies in this regard, and that of Perroni is a characteristic example, confront this research with a 'traditionsgeschichtlich' approach, that is in the attempt of reconstructing that which was the concrete historical ecclesial frame in which the literary traditions were formed and then flowed into the Lucan work. Without negating the interest and the plausibility of such methodology, I retained an approach instead of examining the text at the redactional level; that is to study how the figures of the woman are inserted in the theological-literary composition of the final redactor of the Acts of the Apostles. From this point of view it is fundamental to identify precisely the aim and therefore the literary structure of the Acts. To this end the study of G. Betori[3] makes an illuminating contribution. In conclusion of research into the book of Acts that lasted more than twenty years, the author proposes a structure, a chiastic configuration, that one can schematise as follows:[4]

Introduction: 1:1–14

1st Part: 1:12–8:4 (in Jerusalem)

2nd Part: 8:1b-14:28 (Palestine and Asia Minor)

3rd Part: 14:27–16:5 (Council of Jerusalem)

4th Part: 15:35–19:22 (Acaia and Asia Minor)

5th Part: 19:20–28:31 (Jerusalem and Rome)

Conclusion: 28:14b-31

As is seen in this scheme, the book sets out the progressive 'extension of the announcement of salvation to the pagans' and the 'relationship between this extension and the role of Israel'.[5] These themes are the content borne by the whole book and reveal its intention. As the apostle Paul says in the conclusion, verse 28:28, 'Let it be known to you then that the salvation of God has been sent to the Gentiles'. Following the indication of Jesus recalled at the beginning of the work (Acts 1:8: 'you shall receive power when the Holy Spirit has come upon you; and you shall be my witnesses in Jerusalem and in all Judea and Samaria and to the end of the earth'), the Acts tell of the progressive overcoming of every geographic and cultural barrier that the Word of God, through the power of the Holy Spirit, completes, in successive stages, until reaching Rome, the centre of the world at that time and therefore 'the end of the earth'. But this universal extension is not achieved while denying or abandoning the origin, the history, the past, the promise of God; rather it reclaims it in a broader perspective, integrating it into a more expansive organism. The return in the fifth part of the book to Jerusalem is also indicative of this, before making the great journey to Rome.

The centre point and the central dynamic of this universal openness is the Council of Jerusalem (Ch. 15), in the centre of the chiasmic structure, in which we are told of the anguished decision making which, under the action of the Holy Spirit, carried the universal dimension of the nascent Church to official and definitive sanction. As the apostle Peter says in v. 15:11, 'we believe that we shall be saved through the grace of the Lord Jesus, just as they will.' One can also see how the centrality of chapter 15 divides the whole of Acts into two large blocks: in the first (chs. 1–14) the protagonist is principally Peter, while in the second (chs. 16–28) the scene is dominated by the apostle Paul. Peter represents the link with the past, with the historical event of Jesus that he walked with his own people in the streets of Palestine. Paul represents the post-Easter novelty and documents the permanent action of the risen Christ and His presence in the life of the Church that ever opens new geographic and cultural horizons. Both of the apostles are in any case protagonists of an agenda of universal openness and exactly the 'handover', from one to the other, illustrates the fundamental theme of the broadening of the perspective in the continuity of the source.

The question that is posed at this point is the following: What presence is assigned to the women in this triumphant journey of the Word of God? Of the numerous female figures only the principal ones are here analyzed. These are located, by an artificial composition that is probably not casual, in 6 pericopes, spread according to a concentric structure that rotates around chapter 15:

1. The community in expectation of the Spirit (1:12–14) (A)

2. The wonderworking of Peter in Judea (9:32–43) (B)

3. The liberation of Peter from prison (Chapter 12) (C)

4. The liberation of Paul and Silas from prison (16:11–40) (C')

5. The evangelization of Achaia and Asia Minor by Paul (18:1–19:20) (B')

6. The visit of Paul to Caesarea (21:1–16) (A')

As can be seen we are not dealing here with pericopes which have as their protagonists feminine figures. Rather, we are dealing with episodes that have as their principal actors the apostles. However, as will be seen, the feminine figures here present have a most significant importance that merits being highlighted.

The community in expectation of the Spirit

As has already been seen, the first part of Acts comprises the chapters 1:12–8:4. This in turn can be divided in two sections: 1:12–2:47; 2:42–8:4. These demonstrate, respectively, the constitution and the life of the Christian community.[6] In the first section we pass 'from a group still unformed, that described in Acts 1:12–14, to a true community in the fullness of its own life, described in Acts 2:42–47, thanks to the constitution of the apostolic college (Acts 1:15–16) and of the Church animated by the Spirit (Acts 2:1–41)'.[7] As Betori[8] notes, 'the presentation of the personalities, in 1:13–14, is constructed as an imperfect parallelism: after two series in which appear four personalities, follow two series of only three personalities or groups of them. The gaps in the third and the fourth series wait, obviously, for completion which comes, respectively, with the reconstruction of the college of the twelve, through the election of Matthias (1:15–26), and with the enlargement of the group of disciples, fruit of the Pentecost (2:1–41). The entire transition represented by 1:12–14 thus appears projected towards the future, of which it constitutes a premise and almost a justification.' Given this strict connection between vv. 1:13–14 and 2:1–41, it is not possible to ignore the parallelism found here between all of this first section of Acts and the beginning of the gospel of Luke (Luke 1:26–38), where we are told how Mary becomes the 'mother of Jesus' (Acts 1:14), of that descendant of David of whom Peter, full of the Holy Spirit, announces the enthronement during the day of Pentecost.[9] 'The Holy Spirit will come upon you, and the power of the Most High will overshadow you' said the angel to Mary (Luke 1:35). 'You shall receive power when the Holy Spirit has come upon you; and you shall be my witnesses […] to the end of the earth' (Acts 1:8) said Jesus, predicting the event of Pentecost.

Just as the Spirit generated the descendant of David in the womb of Mary, so now, descending on this group of people gathered around her, He opens it to a universal perspective. The seed of the eschatological community is sown here, that community which embraces all the people of the earth (Acts 2:9–11). Thus once again the mystery of the virginal conception by the work of the Holy Spirit is fulfilled: 'The Holy Spirit will come upon you, and the power of the Most High will overshadow you'.[10]

Peter in Judea (9:32–43)

The second part of the Acts (8:1b-14:28) tells of the first spreading of the word of the gospel outside Jerusalem. It is divided into three sections, dedicated respectively to the Hellenists (8:1b-9:31), to Peter (9:31–12:24) and to Saul and Barnabas (12:24–14:28). The second stage tells of the apostolic action of Peter along the Mediterranean coast and reaches its high point in the baptism of the pagan Cornelius, 'episode of extreme importance for the author of Acts, who in this context repeats the narration twice and makes of it a decisive element in the Assembly of Jerusalem. But the centrality of Peter in this section is emphasized also from his return on the scene in Jerusalem through his miraculous liberation from imprisonment.'[11]

The question that is posed is the following: how is this openness to the pagans possible? And in particular, how was Peter able, this man who had never eaten anything impure (cf 10:14), to go into the house of the uncircumcised? The first impulse was certainly given by persecution which caused an initial dispersion of the believers in Christ.[12] The visit of Peter to the cities on the coast is probably to be placed in connection with that initial evangelization (9:32). In fact, going to Lydda, Peter begins his journey towards Caesarea. He begins here, with the healing of Aeneas, to make present the therapeutic force of Jesus outside of Jerusalem.[13] But while Peter was in Lydda, still further north, at Joppa, a disciple named Tabitha died. Immediately they sent to call Peter, even though we realize that this expansion of his journey does not seem to be something obviously desirable for him. The disciples therefore had to exhort him with decision: 'Please come to us without delay (*me okneses)*' (v. 38b). The verb *'okneo'* appears only once in the New Testament, but in Numbers 22:16 the same call to overcome every delay ('let nothing hinder you in coming to me') is addressed by the king Balak to the fortune-teller Balaam, whom God had prohibited from going to curse the elected people as Balak wanted. There is therefore a significant obstacle that needs to be overcome, but Peter rises anyway and goes with the messengers.

The brief but dense description of the good works and almsgiving that Tabitha was doing that introduced the episode, acts perhaps as justification for this condescension of Peter. In fact this description foreshadows that of Cornelius 'a devout man who […] gave alms liberally to the people.' (Acts 10:2). Widows are then presented as surrounding the figure of Tabitha, crying and showing 'tunics and other garments which Dorcas [Tabitha] made _while she was with them_' (v.39), highlighting once again the merits of the deceased. Peter finally consents, puts himself to prayer, recalls Tabitha to life, calls the saints and the widows and presents her to them alive (*zosan*). It is significant that the expression underlined used to describe Tabitha is used twice in the gospel for Jesus: 'Why do you seek the living [*zonta*] among the dead?

He is not here but has risen. Remember how he told
you *while he was still* in Galilee' (Luke 24:5f; cf 24:44:
'These are my words which I spoke to you, *while I was
still with you*'). Also significant is the recurrence of the
verb 'to rise' in this pericope. If at first the invitation
turned to Aeneas by Peter ('rise and make your bed'
v.34), then it is Peter himself that 'rose' (v. 39) in order
to go to Joppa, where he repeats the invitation to rise
to Tabitha (v. 40). This movement seems preparatory
to the invitation that Peter himself heard on the roof
of the house of Simon the tanner during the vision,
'Rise, Peter; kill and eat' (10:13). It is a movement
towards a new life, that Christ sustains, re-animating
the sick and the dead and leading his Church towards
greater horizons. This perspective will be consecrated
by the call of the angel to the imprisoned Peter: 'get up
('rise') quickly' (12:7) with which he sent him on the
road towards freedom.

Reposing the initial question, we can say that Peter
arrived at Caesarea thanks to the presence on his way
of two figures Aeneas and Tabitha, who progressively
led his away from Jerusalem, setting him off towards
that place fundamental for the openness of the Christian mission: Caesarea. Aeneas and Tabitha constitute
a pair, but it is clear that in the construction of the story
the emphasis falls on Tabitha, living in Joppa. It is at
Joppa in fact, in the house of Simon the tanner, that
Peter has the decisive vision that will prepare him to
accept the invitation of the messengers from the
centurion Cornelius. The way towards the entrance of
the house of Cornelius is marked by spaces, by inter-
mediary stages: the disciple Tabitha and the group of
widows gathered around her constitute, in fact, that
determinant ring of association that allows for making

the leap from the known to the unknown, from the district of Jerusalem towards the cosmopolitan cities of the coast, from the world of the circumcised to that of the uncircumcised. The disciple Tabitha, not with words, but with her work, made possible this crossing, a step between two hitherto irreconcilable worlds.

Peter is liberated from Prison (12:1–24)

The baptism of Cornelius inaugurated 'officially the ecumenical openness of the Christian mission over-coming the cultural restrictions and the religious barriers of Judaism'.[14] Subsequently Peter has to make this fact acceptable to the community of Jerusalem (11:1–18) and therefore the narrative introduces an additional expansion of the gospel with the coming to Antioch of the Christians expelled from Jerusalem, as if to confirm that the direction opened by Peter was the right one (11:19–30). At this point, like a symbolic coronation of all the initiatives taken by Peter, the story of his nocturnal liberation from prison is told. The account of the liberation (vv. 12: 6–17) is inserted in the middle of two sections that present the persecutor Herod in his action against the Church (vv. 12: 1–5) and in his death (vv. 12: 18–24). The incarceration of Peter is located in the middle of greater hostilities, in particular on the part of the Jews, and takes place, like that of Jesus, in the approach to Passover. It is in fact during the Passover night that he achieves liberation, while the Church is in prayer.

The story is divided into 3 parts:
A) The Liberation from prison (6–10)
B) The reflection of Peter (11–12)
C) The entrance into the house of Mary (13–17)

In the first part (6–10: the liberation) verbs typical of
Exodus are noted: *exerchomai* (to exit) vv. 7–10 (cf. 7:3,
4, 7); *akoloutheo* (to follow) vv. 8–9; *exago* (lead out) v.
17 (cf. 7: 36,40). Even the liberating angel recalls the
angel promised by God to his people, because he
precedes them and guides them along the way towards
the promised land (Ex 23:20–23; cf. 14:19). One can also
note the theme of the nocturnal intervention and the
light which also refer to the crossing of the Red Sea (Ex
14), above all in its symbolic restatement in the book
of Wisdom (ch 10:17–18).[15]

In the third part (13–17), symmetrical to the first, the
entrance into the house of Mary is described; in order
to enter that dwelling it is necessary that a door be
opened (v. 16, cf. v. 10). The binary structure (exit-enter)
of the exodus epic thus comes to its completion.[16]

In the central part, (vv. 11–12) Peter is by himself
and experiences the moment of his full awakening.[17]
Here he at first looks back to the liberation completed
by the Lord through his angel, and then he moves with
decisiveness in order to go to the house of Mary.
Rightly a parallel is seen between Ex 18:4 (Septuagint),
when Moses recalls his liberation ('The God of my
father was my help and delivered me from the sword
of Pharaoh') and the words that Peter himself says:
'the Lord has sent his angel and rescued me from the
hand of Herod' (Acts 12:11; see also Acts 7:10)[18]. The
event of the liberation has therefore two aspects: the
liberation from prison and the entrance into the house
of Mary, which correspond almost in equal measure
even in terms of the magnitude of the story.[19]

But the entrance into the house of Mary is marked
in its turn by the episode of Rhoda, the young maid
that recognized the voice of Peter. Although she does

not open the door immediately, she goes anyway to announce the presence of Peter to the others. Her intervention, granted with a term a little derogatory ('*maine*', delirious), in fact has a precursory function, that of a preannouncement, akin to that of other women in the gospel of Luke: Elizabeth, who encountering Mary anticipates the Christological confession of Peter (1:43); the women at the tomb on the morning of Easter, whose announcement was not believed by the apostles but considered a delirium (*leros*) (Lk 24:11). Also Rhoda, after running, told [announced] (v. 14) that Peter was at the door, anticipating that which Peter himself will say immediately after, 'Tell [announce] this to James and to the brethren [of his liberation and work of the Lord]' (v. 17). With subtle irony, Luke inserts between these two verbal forms of the verb to 'announce' (or tell) in vv. 14 and 17, the noun 'It is his (Peter's) angel (*anghelos*)' (v. 15). In such a way, that which is a sceptical reaction of the gathered faithful becomes in fact an implicit recognition of the role of Rhoda: not 'the angel of Peter' is at the door, but Rhoda is 'the angel of Peter'. Rhoda anticipates that proclamation of the liberating act of God that the protagonist Peter will subsequently make to those present. In this sense, we can say that Rhoda has a symmetrical role to that of the angel of the Lord in the first part of the story. The angel of the Lord ordered Peter to follow him in order to exit the door of the prison; Rhoda preceded Peter into the house of Mary, in order to precede the announcement of his liberation.

A final note ought to be made from the point of view of the terminology of Exodus. Peter, after having asked for the event to be told to James, 'departed [*exelthon*]' to another place (v. 17). The house of Mary is not a

definitive dwelling place, it is only a temporary lodg-
ing: the exodus of Peter continues.[20]

After the death of the persecutor Herod (vv. 18–23),
the story concludes with the words: 'the word of God
grew and multiplied' (v. 24). Thus is revealed the
global meaning of the section: the persecution threat-
ened to block, to incarcerate the word of God, the
testimony of the Church. The miraculous intervention
of God reopens the door and the Word renews its way
towards the entire world. On the one hand is held 'all
that the Jewish people were expecting' (v. 11) that had
already expressed itself in the murder of Stephen
(chapter 7) and that tends to block the diffusion of the
Word of God; on the other hand is held the force of the
Spirit, the power of God that guides Peter towards the
pagans and liberates him from the distress of prison;
this last evokes by symbolic analogy the yoke of the
law, which 'neither our fathers nor we have been able
to bear…But we believe that we shall be saved through
the grace of the Lord Jesus, just as they will' (15:10).
Peter will speak in this way at the Council of Jerusalem, thus sanctioning definitively that condition of
liberty that the Lord had made him experience symbolically liberating him from the chains of prison.

In this frame the 'house of Mary' also assumes a
particular value. The verses of the central section
(11–12) are arranged in an antithetical parallelism:

v. 11: 'And Peter came to himself and said: "Now I am sure
that the Lord has sent his angel
and rescued me from the *hand of Herod*
and from all that the Jewish people were expecting."'

v. 12: 'When he realized this,
he went to the *house of Mary*, the mother of John whose other
name was Mark,

where many were gathered together
and were praying.'

As one can see, the 'hand of Herod' (from which Peter
is liberated), is contrasted with the 'house of Mary' (into
which Peter enters). And like the hand of Herod is the
place in which 'all that the Jewish people were expecting' takes shape, so the house of Mary is the place in
which 'many were gathered together' (the new people
of God) 'praying': the true attitude of expectation. It
emphasizes how instead of the 'Jewish people', which
suggests a precise and limited ethnic reality, there is
placed a group of people, determined only by the divine
subject that gathers them and to whom they turn in
prayer[21]. But, above all, we need to stress how against
the hand of Herod, symbol of oppression and of slavery,
there is placed in contraposition the house of Mary,
symbol of the land of freedom, towards which the tribe
of Abraham (cf. 7:3) is always on a journey. Naturally,
in as much as it is a symbol, it is not a definitive reality,
as is clearly illustrated by the final phrase, '[Peter]
departed and went to another place.' (v.17).

As Herod synthesizes in a person all of the forces
opposed to the freedom of the Word of God, so Mary
is the person that represents symbolically all those that
are gathered by the force of the Word of God and
entrust themselves to it in prayer. The exodus from
distress of the Jewish people does not mean autono-
mistic isolation or a meander without a goal, but entry
into a community of those who, persevering in prayer,
were staying together and breaking bread from house
to house (2:42–46). The figure of Mary gives a personal
face to this welcoming community. She moreover is
presented as the mother of John, also known as Mark,
a person who will be cited at the end of the pericope,

in the summary of v. 25, in which we are presented with, 'the protagonists of the new way of the gospel, the team of the first missionary journey into the world of the pagans: Barnabas, Saul and the assistant collaborator John Mark'.[22] The name of this woman, symbol of the welcoming dwelling place, is thus also strictly connected to the universal missionary perspective, confirming the fact that the community is not a place of refuge for its own end, that would re-create in an even smaller way the closed ethnicity of the' Jewish people', but it is an open community, missionary, with its eyes turned towards the ends of the earth. The maternity of Mary, here recalled, highlights her capacity of reception, but above all of extending outwards, of 'giving birth' to the spaces of the universal mission.

From this point of view, Rhoda, with her precursory announcement, represents the inner soul of the entire story. She assumes the role of the angel of the Lord, demonstrating how no closed door is able to stop the announcement of the work of the Lord. Rhoda 'did not open the gate' but took the message inside; with her comes in anticipation the announcement that Peter brings.

In conclusion, if the story tells of the liberation of Peter, symbol of the liberty that God confers in His Word, it is evident that Peter is preceded, received and pushed forward by Rhoda and by Mary. The vocation of the women in the journey of the gospel to the ends of the earth is thus manifested.

Paul is liberated from Prison (16:11–40)

'With the problems connected to the journey of the gospel to the pagan world resolved, the Acts turn themselves to the description of the mission that Paul leads in the new territories to the west (Acts 15:36–19:22)'.[23] In a first phase the missionaries work in Macedonia and in Achaia (16:6–18:23) and in a second stage in the province of Asia (18:18–19:22). The first step of the mission in Europe is Philippi, where Paul and Silas experience liberation from prison has several similarities with that of Peter (16:11–40). However, while the episode relative to Peter is located almost as an emblematic conclusion to the part of the Acts that it concerns, the liberation of Paul and Silas is located practically at the start of their mission, thereby indicating the underlying characteristics that will distinguish it.[24]

The telling of the stay of the missionaries at Philippi which focuses on the nocturnal liberation from prison is divided into 5 parts, set out concentrically:

A (11–15): exit from the city

B (16–22): liberation of the soothsayer

C (23–27): divine intervention

B' (28–34): salvation of the jailer

A' (35–40): exit from prison

The first scene (vv. 11–15) develops according to a technique of progressively shrinking the horizons; it presents first of all the city of Philippi (vv. 11–12), then the missionaries that go out on the Sabbath day and the group of women in prayer outside the gate to the city (v. 13) and finally a woman, Lydia, who, baptized with her household, encouraged the two missionaries to come into her house, as the disciples of Emmaus had done with Jesus (vv. 14ff; cf. Luke 24:29). The fundamental movement is therefore still, like in ch 12, that of the exodus, of the exit by a gate (16:13; cf. 12:10) in

70 Peter and Magdalen

order to enter into the house of a woman (cf. 12:12). This fundamental movement is found again in the fifth scene (35–40), where Paul and Silas, 'when it was day', were invited to 'come out' (v. 36), then 'they took them out' (v. 39 cf. 12:17) and finally, 'went out' from prison, they visited Lydia and exited in the end definitively after having greeted the brethren (v. 40; cf. 12:17).

At the centre of the pericope (25–27) comes the divine intervention: in the middle of the night (cf. Wisdom 18:14), while Paul and Silas are praying (cf. 16:13; 12:5, 12) a 'sudden' earthquake (cf. 2:2) opens the gate of the prison.[25]

The second scene (16–24) tells of the liberation of a young (slave) soothsayer, from whom Paul, invoking the name of Jesus, forces out a spirit of divination. This fact though is preceded by a prophetic statement of the woman concerning the two missionaries: 'These men are servants of the Most High God, who proclaim to you the way of salvation' (v. 17).[26] There follows a parallel declaration of the girl's patrons: 'These men are Jews and they are disturbing our city. They advocate customs which it is not lawful for us Romans to accept or practice' (vv. 20f). The way of salvation is thus presented: it is liberation from a spirit of oppression and of slavery and the announcement instead of new ways of life; these ways though contrast with the authorities of the city who therefore throw the missionaries into prison (v. 23).

The fourth scene (28–34) tells, in parallel with the second, of the way of salvation of the jailer. In contrast to the patrons (*'kurioi'*) of the young girl, who do not want to do that which Paul and Silas announce, the jailer asks them, 'Men [*kurioi*] what must I do to be saved?' And they said, 'Believe in the Lord Jesus […]'

(vv. 30f). The same Lord Jesus that liberated the young girl from the spirit, saves the jailer, with his family, who after baptism hastens to have Paul and Silas come up to his house (cf v. 15).[27]

Even the mission of Paul in Europe therefore begins with an exodus; the exodus has God as its fundamental protagonist, invoked in nocturnal prayer; realized at first realistically as an exit, symbolically dense, from the city, that does not want to welcome the way of salvation, the new morality,[28] and then as a real escape from prison in which the leaders of the city wish to restrict, to block the Word of the Lord. If the ultimate cause of this exodus is God who works the nocturnal wonder, we need to stress no less that, as the proximate cause which allows for the escape of the two apostles from prison there are the leaders of the city, so in a similar way the proximate cause that allowed the missionaries to leave the city is the group of women gathered 'outside the gate to the riverside'. The way of salvation, the way towards liberty has, therefore, in this group of women an enthralling foretaste.

The word of the Lord which cannot be enchained is also the way of salvation for all: it gives liberty first to the young slave girl soothsayer, making the spirit exit from her, and then to the jailer who is then baptized.

We need finally to note that the missionaries of the Word leaving a restrictive place, enter again into the house of Lydia, which is thus made, from a literary-structural point of view, like the promised land, the land of liberty,[29] the land where the way of salvation is received, where the new customs are practised.[30] However, even in this case, we are not dealing with a permanent dwelling place, but only a partial anticipation and therefore the missionaries, after having exhorted the brothers, 'departed' from the house (v. 40).

Thus the mission of Paul from the beginning is under the sign of the power of the Word of God, which escapes from the snares of the city of men, who do not want to receive the way of salvation, and finds space instead in the heart of the one who believes, first Lydia and then of the jailer.[31] In the dynamic of salvation the women have therefore an anticipatory and pre-figurative role, whether preceding the path of the Word of the Lord, being the first to receive it or indicating in an anticipatory way its salvific role.

It is meaningful from this point of view to note the parallelism between this episode and the welcome, given by Rahab, to the two explorers of the people of Israel, which chapter two of the book of Joshua describes. In a similar way, here, we are dealing with two men venturing into a new region for the first time, into a hostile city; analogously with Acts 16 they are welcomed by a woman into a house of this city. And this woman also first professes faith in the God of Israel and then involves in this conversion her entire household, as does Lydia.

Paul in Corinth and Ephesus (18:1–19:20)

If the first stage of Paul's mission in Europe was Philippi, passing through Thessalonica, Beroea and Athens, it reaches its conclusive stage in Corinth (18:1–23). Here Paul meets the couple Aquila and Priscilla, who will accompany him in the mission to Ephesus (18:24–19:20). In this missionary activity of Paul, told through these 'dramatic episodes',[32] one can see a certain parallel with the analogous missionary activity of Peter in the second part of Acts (chs. 8–14).

꧁꧂

The first collaboration of Paul with Aquila and Priscilla (18:1–23) is divided into 5 parts:

A (1–4): preaching in the synagogue of Corinth

B (5–8): separation with the Jews of the synagogue

C (9–11): encouragement of the Lord to preach

B' (12–17): tribunal before Gallio

A' (18–23): preaching in the synagogue of Ephesus

The first and the fifth scene are characterized by the mention of Aquila and Priscilla. The first scene (1–4) tells of the coming of Paul to Corinth and more precisely to stay with Aquila and Priscilla (1–2); his stay with them and his preaching in the synagogue (3–4) while doing so. The fifth scene (18–23), in a way different to the first which is characterized by a long stay ('he stayed with them', v. 3), is marked by a great movement, initially in the company of the married couple, in two structured series of parallel activity:

I—Departure from Corinth (v. 18), arrival at Ephesus and preaching in the synagogue (v. 19), refusal to remain there for a long time (v. 20).

II—Departure from Ephesus (v. 21), arrival at Caesarea and greeting to the Church (v. 22), departure after a brief time (v. 23).

The central scene (9–11) contains the exhortation of the Lord during the night (cf. 12:6; 16:25) to Paul, in order that he would continue to announce the Word of God, despite the difficulties that possibly intimidate him.

The second and the fourth scenes tell of the difficulties between Paul and the Jews. The second scene (5–8) tells of the consequences of Paul's preaching: separation from the Jews, the conversion of many Corinthians and of the ruler of the synagogue. The fourth scene (12–17) tells of the complaint of the Jews against Paul in the tribunal of Gallio (12–13), the refusal of Gallio to make judgment (14–16) and the anger of the Jews against the ruler of the synagogue in the tribunal of Gallio (17–18).

The ultimate protagonist of the preaching of the Word is therefore the Lord who, precisely in full darkness and difficulties, does not cease from encouraging Paul to continue in his mission of teaching the Jews and the Greeks the Word of God, debating with them in the synagogue. Paul develops this mission with greater calm in Corinth (v. 11, cf. Luke 24:49)[33] and in more of a hurry in Ephesus, Caesarea, Antioch, Galatia and Phrygia. His mission is continuously obstructed by the hostility of the Jews but nevertheless gives rise to a triumph for the nascent community.

Against this background the pair of Aquila and Priscilla takes on a certain importance. Luke takes care in fact to highlight that if underlying and at the centre of the entire mission is the encouragement of the Lord, the activity of debating in the synagogue basically begins to develop from the moment in which Paul, having found these two engaged in the same trade, takes up living with them. In a similar way the subsequent journey that will take him to continue the same activity of debating in the synagogue in Ephesus, occurs still in the company of the same couple, to whom Paul appears linked both in his stable mission and in his travelling work. We need moreover to note that while v. 3 says that Paul 'stayed' with them, in v. 20 it is stated that Paul did not accept an invitation 'to stay' much time with the Jews 'when they asked him to stay for a longer period'. Therefore the choice of Paul to live with Aquila and Priscilla is proposed in a way that gives it particular emphasis and identify it as a preferential option of Paul with regard to the married couple. Such a decision, recalled in the central section with the verb *'ekathisen'* (*'he stayed* a year and six months, teaching the word of God among them' v. 11), is here clearly placed in relationship with the encouragement received from the Lord.

In the company of Aquila and Priscilla, with whom he was living, in whose house therefore he had the nocturnal vision and who travel with him, the presence of the Lord 'with him' (v. 10), guarantee of every protection and ultimate foundation of the mission, finds the context in which it is made better present; even if, significantly, towards the end of the story Paul, having reached Ephesus, leaves them (v. 19). The course of the Word in fact is not linked in an absolute way to any personal agreement, even the most beneficial. As it turns out, this separation is only temporary and will be an occasion to give better emphasis to the missionary role of the couple in their activity in Ephesus. On the other hand we must also note that while Paul has the support of living with the couple, he experiences two important events: in the first place the transition to the Pagans and the conversion of many of them after the refusal of the Jews, and in the second place the recognition of political innocence and therefore the authorization to continue in the mission on the part of the Roman authorities.[34]

The Second Collaboration of Paul with Aquila and Priscilla (18:24–19:20) is divided into 3 parts:

A (18:24–28): Priscilla, Aquila and Apollos

B (19:1–10): Paul and the disciples of John

A' (19:11–20): The demoniac and the sons of Sceva

The pericope deals with the believers in Jesus in Ephesus and of three cases of imperfect understanding of the way of the Lord (Apollos, the disciples of John and the sons of Sceva) who are helped to deepen the way of God by others (Priscilla and Aquila, Paul, the demoniac).

The episode of Apollos and that of the sons of Sceva have various parallel elements and serve to frame the central episode of Paul, the first in a preparatory positive way, contrasting the second. In the two cases it is underlined that the understanding of the baptism of John or that of Jesus announced by Paul is insufficient. In the first case, Priscilla and Aquila take Apollos to the side and, 'expounded to him the way of God more accurately.' In the second case, the insufficiency of the sons of Sceva, who wish to imitate Paul, are unmasked by the violent aggression of a man possessed by an evil spirit who exposes the alleged exorcists making them flee.

Looking at the first scene, in what does the greater 'accuracy' in the way of God consist? Negatively it is said that Apollos only knew 'the baptism of John'. Positively it is noted that Apollos, after he received instruction, reached Corinth and 'he greatly helped those who through grace had believed' (v. 27). We note the parallel with 15:11: 'we believe that we shall be saved through the grace of the Lord Jesus'. It seems to be the same formulation, even if a more summary form of the process of salvation: it is grace that allows for belief and therefore of being saved (cf. Gal 2:15–21). Apollos, after receiving instruction, adds many to those who 'through grace had believed [that they were saved]'; he was able therefore to contribute further and in a significant way to that free movement for which the Corinthians had come to trust themselves to the mercy of God who saves them. Such an outcome is moreover emphasized by the consequences of the aggression of the demoniac to the sons of Sceva. When the news reaches the inhabitants of Ephesus, 'fear fell upon them all; and the name of the Lord Jesus was extolled. Many also of those who were now believers came, confessing and divulging their practices.' Here also there is an advancement of believers, but dictated rather by a reverential fear in the face of a dominating force (cf. vv 16–20) than by a benevolent mercy. In conclusion, while the baptism of John (18:25) was an invitation to penance (cf. v. 19:4), the way of God espoused with more accuracy highlights the gift, the grace of God.[35]

We can now ask ourselves: how much of the 'graceful' effect of the instruction of the couple is owed to the content of their catechesis and how much to the discreet and welcoming style adopted by them? While Apollos was speaking in public in the synagogue, Priscilla and Aquila took him to one side (*proselabonto*); the verb means 'to take someone with himself'; it is rare in the gospels[36] but is more common in the Acts (5 times). It is used in the case of taking food (twice) and on another occasion has a conspiratorial use (17:5), in each case it suggests a gesture that is discreet and careful. The case of 28:2 is significant, 'the natives showed us unusual kindness, for they kindled a fire and welcomed us all, because it had begun to rain and was cold.' This case recalls the other four passages in the New Testament (Romans 14:1–3; 15:7; Philemon 17), in which the aspect of welcoming is strongly emphasized: 'welcome one another, therefore as Christ has welcomed you' (Romans 15:7). In conclusion it seems that before oral exposition, it was important for the growth of Apollos to have been welcomed with humanity and discretion into the friendship of Priscilla and Aquila; cordiality of a welcome that expresses itself also in the subsequent attitude of the brothers who write to the disciples of Corinth instructing them to receive him (v. 27).

The uniqueness of the intervention of the two emerges also from the comparison with that of Paul in confronting the people who were in the same situation as Apollos. Paul challenges directly the disciples of John while Priscilla and Aquila first listen to Apollos preaching. Paul *places* his hands *over* them, the two *expound* to him the way, they make a proposal. They announce the way of salvation. Paul gives, the two offer a possibility. Naturally we are dealing with two complementary aspects of the mystery and of the Christian mission; two aspects that at the same time are revelatory of the personality of the proponents.

The central intervention of Paul, through the imposition of hands by which the Holy Spirit descends on the disciples of John, is a focal point which hinges on a journey of deepening of the 'way of God'. If the second section of this part of the Acts of the Apostles (chapters 16 to 18) was dedicated to the initial announcement of the Word, this third section is rather dedicated to the progression of those disciples who believed (cf. 18:27; 19:2, 8) or at least had already a certain understanding of the way of the Lord (18:25; 19:15). In such a way Luke is able also to present the activity of Paul as that of one who 'is maker of unity'.[37] As for the content of this deepening, Luke, while underlining the central role of the action of the Holy Spirit, stresses first of all the importance of a more precise knowledge of the way of God, and then makes evident certain practical consequences: the healing of the sick, the confession of sins, the abandonment of magic arts, and the detachment from money.

Also in this activity, like in that of the preceding section, the Word is the protagonist, that 'grew and prevailed mightily' (vv. 19–20). If this growth and re-enforcement of the Word culminates in the gift of the Holy Spirit (the third Pentecost), it nevertheless has its beginning, before all, with a more accurate exposition of the way of God, and then becomes explicit in the moral conversion of the believers. In this frame, Priscilla and Aquila have a role of recalling— the first step of every spiritual deepening or re-enforcement of chains of unity: the welcoming and catechesis. Naturally, the gift of the Holy Spirit and the conversion are necessary but these flourish in the context of a welcome that directs in the way of grace. The parallel between this journey and that which is told of Cornelius in chapter 10 is significant. Also in his case, before the Holy Spirit comes down on him and he is baptized, Peter teaches him about Jesus, 'beginning from Galilee after the baptism which John preached' (v. 10:37; cf. 18:25).

The ministry of Paul, in this fourth part of the Acts, started with the welcome into the house of Lydia and analogously finds its conclusion with Priscilla and Aquila. This couple on the one hand offered him a place to live in Corinth, the base for a period of profitable missionary activity and then accompanied him on the first mission to Ephesus, creating that context in which the presence and the comfort of Jesus was made present to encourage the mission while it was in the middle of trials. On the other hand, they introduced with a discreet and precise style, the missionary activity of Paul in Ephesus and in particular the gift of the Spirit by the imposition of his hands. Priscilla and Aquila, taking aside and instructing Apollos, concretely demonstrated to him how the way of the Lord is grace, a gift that changes the one who receives it in faith.

How much can the activity of the couple be attributed to Priscilla rather than to Aquila? When we first encounter the couple (18:1) the male, Aquila, is named first, understandably so since here we are introduced for the first time to a married couple expelled from Rome; but already, in the section that concludes the pericope (18:18), Priscilla precedes Aquila in an inversion which is apparently unjustified, unless to indicate that she has now assumed a more prevalent role. In a similar way, also in v. 18:26 Priscilla is named first.[38] It does not seem unjustified then to think that this pre-eminence of the woman might be one of the fundamental reasons for the style of welcome and of grace that characterizes the intervention of the couple, in particular if it is compared with the style of the other two interventions that have male protagonists (Paul and the demoniac).

Paul in Caesarea (21:1–16)

In the final part of the book of Acts, the role of Paul as witness of Jesus is illustrated[39] in two stages, dominated respectively by the city of Jerusalem (19:20–23:11) and that of Rome (23:11–28:31). In the first section first of all the journey that leads Paul to Jerusalem is presented (19:20–21:16) and then the hostilities against him in the city (21:16–23:11). In the first of these two phases, Paul detaches himself from the places and from the people who had seen his preceding missionary activity[40], until he arrives in Caesarea in the house of Philip. The scene (21:7–14) is framed in the middle of a broader description of the whole journey from Ephesus to Jerusalem (21:1–16). Already in the first section (1–8) the story is interrupted by an encounter in Tyre which serves 'to emphasize the determination of Paul in confronting his sorrowful destiny'.[41] Subsequently, the travelers reach Caesarea where the second episode takes place (7–14), in which, 'the revelation of the Holy Spirit reminds readers of the dominant perspective of this journey towards Jerusalem'.[42] The pericope is divided into 3 parts:

A) vv. 7–9: presentation of Philip and of his virgin daughters

B) vv. 10–12: speech of the prophet and the negative reaction

C) vv. 13–14: speech of Paul and the adherence of the community

In this context, F. Bovon has noted a literary scheme present in Greek literature and in the literature of Christian martyrs, according to which relatives and friends seek to dissuade one from the destiny of passion and death, placing themselves in opposition to that of hero or martyr, regarding their particular fate[43]. If this emphasis seems valid, at the same time we cannot but avoid noticing the correspondence between the structure of this story and that of the calling of Mary in chapter 1 of the gospel of Luke:

A) 1:26–27: presentation of the virgin

B) 1:28–34: first speech of the angel and the perturbation of Mary

C) 1:35–38: second speech of the angel and acceptance by Mary

In both cases, moreover, certain common terms are used:

aspasamenoi (having greeted) (Acts 21:7:cf. Luke 1:29);

eiselthontes (entered) (Acts 21:8; cf. Luke 1:28);

parthenoi (virgins) (Acts 21:9; cf. Luke 1:27; these are the only cases in the Lucan works);

to pneuma to aghion (the Holy Spirit) (Acts 21:11; cf. Luke 1:35);

andra (man) (Acts 21:11; cf. Luke 1:34)

onomatos tou Kuriou Iesou (for the name of the Lord Jesus) (Acts 21:13; cf. Luke 1:31)

eipontes tou Kuriou to thelema ghinestho (saying: the will of the Lord be done) [Acts 21:14; cf. Luke 1:38, *eipen de Mariam idou he doule Kuriou, ghenoito moi kata to rema sou* (Mary said: behold the handmaid of the Lord, be it done to me according to your word)]

The hypothesis is therefore that Luke may have wished to place at the beginning of the final decisive stage of the mission of Paul, as a form of inclusion of all his work, a kind of parallel scene to the call of Mary, which of itself principally concerns Paul and his destiny as a witness of Christ. But the structure of the story in three phases, each divided into two parts, assigns a particular role to the group of the four virgin prophetesses. In fact, after the arrival of the travelers at Philip's house (a'), reference is made to the presence there of the four virgins (a''); after the speech of the prophet Agabus (b') reference is made to the negative reaction of those present (*hoi entopioi*) (b''); and finally, after the speech of Paul (c'), reference is made to the adherence of those present (c''). A significant portion of the group of those present at the prophecy on the destiny of Paul is therefore these four daughters of Philip who, being mentioned explicitly at the start of the episode, characterize the entire group in the successive phases. If, therefore, the episode principally concerns Paul and his conformation to Christ, it seems nevertheless that Luke wished to associate with it all the community of the brothers and, in a particular way, the four 'unmarried daughters'. The very fact of mentioning them at the beginning of the scene, with this characteristic that recalls the figure of the Virgin Mary, would seem moreover to suggest that it is precisely their presence which determines the painful but total adherence of the community to the will of God. This communal response, which substantially recalls the words of Mary, continues the attitude of openness and availability to the Lord. Virginity is not therefore only a radical openness to the creating power of God, who with his Word made heaven and earth exist (cf. Gen.

1 and Luke 1:38), but is also radical openness, even
after tiring discernment, to the will of God[44], that is
fulfilled in a passion and death like that of Christ.[45]

In this way the presence of the four virgins becomes
an important element in qualifying the attitude of
those others in the story and therefore of the entire
community that is invited to replicate it under the
action of the Holy Spirit. In this sense, we must note
also the elements of parallelism between this scene and
that of Mary with the apostles in the upper room,
waiting for the Holy Spirit, who will open the community to all the people. The openness and availability of
all those present in Caesarea consecrates the total
adhesion of Paul to his destiny of passion that leads
him to make witness to Christ all the way to Rome, 'to
the ends of the earth' (Acts 1:8).[46]

Like the conception of the Lord happened in a
virginal womb, so his burial, in expectation of the
resurrection, happened in a monument excavated in
rock, in which, 'no one had ever been laid [...]the
women who had come with him from Galilee followed, and saw the tomb, and how his body was laid
[...]' (Luke 23:53–55).[47] Analogously, one can say, as
the new community had its beginning in the upper
room in the presence of the 'mother of Jesus', so the
adhesion of the group of disciples to a destiny of death
'for the name of the Lord Jesus' (Acts 21:13) comes in
the presence of the four virgins. The drama of a sinking
of death, received into a virginal heart, is able to carry
fruit that leavens all the earth (cf. Luke 13:21).

Concluding Reflections

As we are able to note easily, the six episodes we have just analyzed correspond in pairs according to the structure anticipated above. Such correspondence gives greater emphasis to some elements already found in the individual analyses. The gradual extension of salvation, overcoming both the barriers of Judaism and the imperial structures, while it has its official sanction by the Council of Jerusalem, has two decisive moments: at Pentecost and during the stay of Paul at Caesarea. In both cases, in the group challenged by the Holy Spirit, the presence of women in a particular position is stressed. The subsequent openness of the community to a universal perspective and dynamic seems therefore to be propitiated by this feminine presence, of which, either implicitly or explicitly, the virginal character is also mentioned.

On the other hand, the concrete start of the universal mission is characterized both for Peter and for Paul by the presence of two couples (a man and a woman),[48] in which the woman has prevalence (Tabitha, Priscilla). Both the sequence of episodes that from v. 9:32 lead to the end of Chapter 10, and those of chapters 18–19 describe a progressive missionary openness of the two apostles, culminating in a descent of the Holy Spirit. In both cases a man and a woman punctuate this development in the sense of accompanying it in the difficult beginning, of giving it the decisive impulse, of preparing for the coming of the Spirit, but it is undeniable that the role of the feminine figure has a particularly important place.

Finally both the ministry of Peter and that of Paul are marked, the former in the final phase, the latter in the initial, by an event of great symbolic weight: the liberation from prison. If this liberation expresses the irrepressible force of the Word of God, that overcomes every attempt of violent repression such as every racial barrier or institutional structure, we cannot fail to note how in both cases the first port of arrival after the escape from prison is the house of a woman. Both Mary and Lydia offer the two apostles, after their liberation, an immediate refuge, even if temporary, where they are able to renew contact with 'the brothers' and bring them that consolation that comes from the announcement of miracles worked by the Lord.

The Word, chained and liberated, finds in the hospitable houses of these two women an environment of recuperation and revival, almost an anticipation of that Kingdom of God in which one will enter, but only through much tribulation (Acts 14:22),[49] where prayer already unites and makes 'brothers'. In both cases moreover we need to emphasize the presence of a young lady (*paidiske*), who has the function of announcing, in anticipation, and beyond all normal logic,[50] the way of salvation: whether the unexpected liberation of Peter, or the salvific mission of Paul and Silas.

The universal way of salvation, through the complementary mediations of the announcement and of the witness until death, is presented in a constant synergy of male and female. More precisely, the presence of the women seems to favour the universal openness, both in the foundational, original, decisive moments which concern the reception of all of the propulsive force of the Spirit, and in those of the concrete beginnings in which one must overcome the heaviness of consolidated schematics and their connected hostilities. Moreover, the women appear especially capable of welcoming in advance the unfolding of salvation and becoming its privileged announcers. The women are presented again as the place of welcome, of hospitality, offering to the journey of the exodus, a place of refuge, a dwelling, the pre-figuration of the kingdom, of the place of liberty and of universalism; even if it is never definitive, it nevertheless has the capacity to regenerate, to return that impulse that pushes outwards towards the universal spaces.

Finally, it does not seem improbable to attribute to the woman (we think of the figure of Priscilla) a particular capacity of introduction to the mystery of grace, the free action by which the Lord turns to 'all those that believe'.

As far as the virgin state, starting from the figure of the Virgin Mary, discretely re-proposed in the four daughters of Philip, it seems to be presented as the privileged space that the Holy Spirit chooses in order to rouse a full adhesion to His plan of universal salvation.

Wishing to synthesize all of these aspects, one is able to say that in the Acts of the Apostles, the woman appears as the 'dwelling place of liberty': in the sense that she is capable of receiving, safe-guarding but also of advancing the way of salvation.

Thus emerges a characteristic role of the woman that is found in a necessary and complementary reciprocity with that of the man. If it is primarily the man who carries the announcement of universal salvation this is only made possible because it is preceded, received, accompanied and driven by the woman.

From this point of view I am not able to share without reservation the affirmation according to which in the Acts, the women, 'never constitute representative typifications of the position of the woman in the

Church'.[51] In fact there is a typification, even if it does not correspond precisely to ministerial roles.

It seems opportune to note finally how an anthropological reflection of the two genders might be illuminated by the Christian event; it highlights their reciprocal relational nature, but gives them also dynamism and equilibrium. If it is true that the man heads towards the woman, seeks this refuge and this dwelling place, and the woman awaits the man, desires his contribution, it appears on the one hand that their roles are profoundly intertwined (here beyond and regardless of the purely biological perspective); on the other hand both find their meaning and their dignity only in the perspective of a salvation that overcomes them and in the service of which they are both employed. Otherwise the mutual dependence would be suffocating. It is only in the perspective of the salvation offered freely by God to everyone that man is able to give himself and trust himself faithfully to the woman in order to give and receive help, and the woman is able to receive the gift of the man and offer to him her help, certain of not being exploited.

The mystery of salvation, already in its propagation through men and women, saves their flesh, their single nature, promoting an ever more creative development: *'et videbit omnis caro salutare Dei'*, 'and all flesh will see the salvation of God' (Luke 3:6).[52]

Notes

1   Cf N. Flanagan, 'The Position of the women in the writings of St. Luke' in *Marianum* 40 (1978). On the subject today see M. Perroni, *Il discepolato delle donne nel vangelo di Luca—un contributo all'ecclesologia neotestamentaria,* Excerptum ex dissertatione ad doctoratum Sacrae Theologiae assequendum in Pontificio Athenaeo S. Anselmi, Roma 1995: specifically chapter II of the thesis, dedicated to the book of the Acts. Here is found also a wide and updated bibliography, to which we can now add: I. Richter Reimer, *Frauen in der Apostelgeschichte des Lukas. Eine feministisch-theologische Exegese,* Mohn, Gutersloh 1992; L. Schottroff, *Lydias ungeduldige Schwestern. Feministische Sozialgeschichte des fruhen Christentums,* Kaiser, Gutersloh 1994; T. K. Seim, *The double Message, Patterns of Gender in Luke-Acts,* Studies of the NT and its World, T and T. Clark, Edinburgh 1994.

2   Perroni, *Il discepolato delle donne nel vangelo di Luca,* p. 8

3   G. Betori, 'La strutturazione del libro degli Atti: una proposta' in *Rivista Biblica* 42 (1994), pp. 3–34.

4   Cf *ibid.,* p. 33.

5   Cf *ibid.,* p. 32.

6   Cf *ibid.,* pp. 9–13.

7   *Ibid.,* p. 10.

8   *Ibid.,* note 13.

9   See the parallel between Luke 1:32 and Acts 2:30.

10   Cf. P. Bossuyt—J. Radermakers, *Temoins de la Parole de la Grace. Actes des Apotres,* Institut d'Etudes Theologiques, Bruxelles 1995, vol. 2, pp. 127 and 275.

11   Betori, 'La strutturazione del Libro degli Atti: una proposta', pp. 14f.

12   M. L. Rigato, '"Mosè e i profeti" in chiave cristiana: un pronunciamento e un midrash (Lc 16:16–18+19–31)' in *Rivista Biblica* 45 (1997), pp. 152 f., notes how from the context one seems obliged to conclude that these 'dispersed' evangelizers (8:1–4) were not only men, but also women.

13   Acts 9:34: 'Aeneas, Jesus Christ heals you; rise'; cf 10:38: 'he went about doing good and healing all'.

14 R. Fabris, *Atti degli apostolic,* Borla, Roma 1977, p. 389.

15 Cf. A. Strobel, 'Passa-Symbolik und Passa-Wunder in Act. XII, 3 ff.' in *New Testament Studies* 4 (1957–58), pp. 210–215.

16 See for example Ex 6:7 f: 'you shall know that I am the Lord your God, who has *brought you out* from under the burdens of the Egyptians. And I will *bring you into* the land which I swore to give to Abraham, to Isaac and to Jacob...'

17 Cf. v. 11 'Now *I am sure...*'; v. 12 'When *he realized* this...'

18 Cf. R. Pesch, *Atti degli apostoli,* Cittadella, Assisi 1987, p. 495

19 Cf J. Roloff, *Die Apostelgeschiche,* Göttingen 1981 (*NTD* 5), p. 187

20 Cf. Bossuyt−Radermakers, *Témoins de la Parole de la Grâce. Actes des Apotres,* p. 391

21 Cf. v. 5: 'earnest prayer for him was made to God by the church', and 2:47, 'And the Lords added to their number day by day those who were being saved.'

22 Fabris, *Atti degli apostoli,* p. 379

23 Betori, 'La strutturazione del libro degli Atti: una proposta', p. 21.

24 Cf. Bossuyt−Radermakers, *Témoins de la Parole de la Grace. Actes des Apotres,* p. 517.

25 Cf. *ibid.* pp. 516 and 618.

26 Cf. Luke 4:34.

27 Cf. Luke 10:30.

28 Cf. Bossuyt−Radermakers, *Témoins de la Parole de la Grace. Actes des Apotres,* pp. 614 and 621.

29 We can think of what Luke says in Acts 14:22: 'through many tribulations we must *enter* the kingdom of God'. Evidently in this step is the symbolism of the exodus, whose goal is the *entrance* into the promised land (cf. also Luke 24:26).

30 Cf. v. 15: 'If you have judged me to be faithful to the Lord'; see also verses 33f: 'he [...] washed their wounds [...] then he brought them up into his house, and set food before them; and he rejoiced with all his household.'

31   Compare Acts 16:14, 'a woman named Lydia [...] the Lord opened her heart [...]' and Luke 10:38f 'a woman named Martha received him into her house. And she had a sister called Mary, who sat at the Lord's feet and listened to his teaching.'

32   Cf. Betori, 'La strutturazione del libro degli Atti: una proposta', p. 23.

33   Cf. Pesch, *Atti degli apostoli*, p. 699.

34   Fabris, *Atti degli apostolic*, p. 543; Bossuyt—Radermakers, *Témoins de la Parole de la Grace. Actes des Apotres*, p. 560.

35   Cf. S. Lyonnet, 'Agape et charismes selon 1 Co. 12:31', in *Paul de Tarse*, Roma 1979, pp. 509–527.

36   Only two cases: for Peter when he takes Jesus to the side, after the prediction of the passion.

37   Cf. Fabris. *Atti degli apostoli*, p. 553: 'the task of Paul is not only that of expanding the Christian movement in a harmonic way but of giving unity and cohesion to all the currents.'

38   On all this question cf. Perroni, *Il discepolato delle donne nel vangelo di Luca*, p. 30.

39   Cf. Betori, 'La strutturazione del libro degli Atti: una proposta', p. 26.

40   *Ibid.*

41   Fabris, *Atti degli apostolic*, p. 604

42   *Ibid.*

43   F. Bovon, 'Le Saint-Esprit, l'Eglise et les relations humaines selon Actes 20:36–21:16' in J. Kremer (ed), *Les Actes des Apôtres. Traditions, rédaction, théologie*, 1979 (*BEThL* 48), pp. 339–358.

44   Cf. Luke 11:2; 22:42; Acts 22:14.

45   Acts 21:11; cf. Luke 18:32; 'The sufferings of Paul are to be seen in the light of Christ's sufferings': see C. M. Martini, *Atti degli Apostoli*, Edizioni Paoline, Roma 1979, p. 278.

46   Cf. Bossuyt—Radermakers, *Témoins de la Parole de la Grace. Actes des Apotres*, p. 611.

47   On this point see also the first chapter.

48   In the two cases, we are dealing with 'operative' people: cf. '*himatia epoiei*' (she made clothes) in 9:39 and '*skenopoioi*' (tentmakers) in 18:3.

49 *'eiselthein eis ten basileian tou theou'* (to enter into the Kingdom of God); cf. Acts 16:15, *'eiselthontes eis ton oikon mou'* (entered into my house); see also Acts 16:40 and 12:12.

50 Cf. Acts 12:15 *'maine'* (you are mad [outside of self] with *'manteuomene'* (guided by the demon) in Acts 16:16.

51 Perroni, *Il discepolato delle donne nel vangelo di Luca*, p. 40, where he cites J. Jervell, 'Die Tochter Abrahams. Die Frau in der Apostelgeschichte' in J. Killunen, *Glaube und Gerechtigkeit. In Memoriam R. Gyllenberg*, Schriften der Finnischen Exegetischen Gesellschaft 38, Helsinki 1983, pp. 90, 83.

52 It is possible to establish an interesting parallel between the dynamic of the book of the Acts and that of *The Trial* of F. Kafka. In both cases we are dealing with a process in which one seeks to escape the logic of a law that dominates everything, tending to block, to close, to suffocate and eventually to kill. In both cases there is also the presence of some feminine figures (in Kafka's book, Frau Grubach, Fraulein Burstner, the wife of the attendant of the tribunal, Leni, the little girls in the house of the painter) who, in different ways, surrounding the event of the protagonist, attempt to open new perspectives, to overcome the restrictions of the law, to soothe the rigour, to deflect the unrelenting application, the bringer of death. But while in *The Trial* the attempts of the women do not have a positive outcome, in the Acts the barrier of the law, thanks to the role done by the women, is overcome, and the Word of the grace reaches all the people.